Praise for *Impact*

"Presenting complex information can be daunting, even for an experienced professional. *Impact* is a must-read for anyone who wants to become a better presenter. Nick Kindler shares coaching tips, tools, and techniques that can help any expert stand out as a thought leader."

DR. MOLLY SHOICHET, award-winning regenerative scientist; former chief scientist of Ontario

"Nick Kindler is a consummate storyteller, engaging communicator, and remarkably effective performance coach. *Impact* is a must-read for all those who stand up, step forward, and hope to share their message successfully with an audience."

JEFF BRADSHAW, founder and executive director, Camp Wenonah and The Camp Wenonah Centre for Outdoor Education; vice president, International Camping Fellowship (ICF)

"In *Impact*, Nick Kindler shares that 'Ideas are the lifeblood of innovation,' and it's true! There is tremendous power in being able to communicate a complex idea. This playbook will help leaders and change-makers better convey and deliver their ideas so they can have a greater impact."

DEBBIE GAMBLE, chief officer, Innovation Labs and New Ventures, Interac

"Whether you are a scientist or a corporate leader, *Impact* is a must-read for anyone wanting to stand out and communicate with impact."

DR. AFSANEH ALAVI, dermatologist, Mayo Clinic

"Nick Kindler's *Impact* is a blueprint for the work that's required to align what you want to say with how you want to be heard."

OREN BERKOVICH, founder and CEO, SingularityU Canada

"For decades I have delivered countless presentations, media interviews, and public speaking engagements from small groups to thousands. Without a doubt, this book's contents have allowed me to create a clearer message, develop better connections, and deliver more impactful communications."

CLINT MAHLMAN, president and chief operating officer, London Drugs

"Nick Kindler is the Communication Whisperer. In *Impact*, Nick shares his secret sauce of how to take complex messages and translate them to approachable, understandable, and actionable stories. This is an essential read for anyone prepping for a presentation or meeting. Okay, strike that. This is an essential read for anyone seeking to communicate with more impact."

TERRY STUART, chief digital officer, Government of Canada at Deloitte Canada

"This book is truly extraordinary. Nick Kindler's approach is simple, powerful, and practical. I have never read a more helpful book on how to communicate with impact and inspire an audience—I can't wait to deliver my next talk using Nick's method."

JODI KOVITZ, founder, #movethedial; Top 100 Most Powerful Women in Canada winner (2017, 2019)

"Nick Kindler's crucial coaching shared in this book will help you craft your knowledge into a talk that really connects with your audience."

FLOYD MARINESCU, CEO and cofounder, C4Media

"Communication: the most important, and potentially most rewarding, act we do throughout every day. Why does it fail so often? Nick Kindler's book is about creating effective and memorable communication. Done correctly, all of our encounters, from social to business, will positively impact our happiness and success. Assuming you want to be better understood, more persuasive, and, yes, impactful, this is a valuable book to enjoy."

MASON HARRIS, founder, speaker, and author of
The Chutzpah Advantage

IMPACT

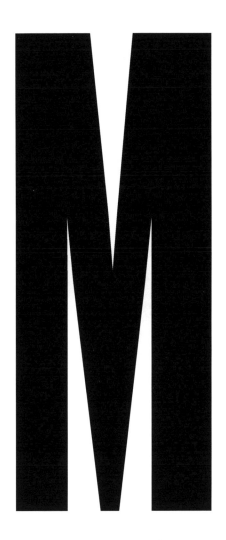

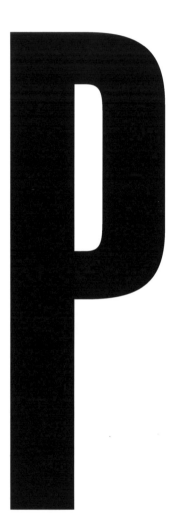

Simplify, Transform,
and Perform Pitches
and Presentations

IMPACT

NICK KINDLER

FOREWORD BY RON TITE

PAGE TWO

Cataloguing in publication information is available from Library and Archives Canada.
ISBN 978-1-77458-110-0 (paperback)
ISBN 978-1-77458-111-7 (ebook)

Page Two
pagetwo.com

Edited by Scott Steedman
Copyedited by Crissy Calhoun
Proofread by Alison Strobel
Cover, interior design, and illustrations by Fiona Lee

impactbook.ca

To my brilliant, beautiful, and loving wife,

Helen Reeve. This is for you.

CONTENTS

FOREWORD

FIRST MET NICK KINDLER in the fall of 1989 while we were both attending Queen's University (*Cha Gheill!*). Before you leap to Google to find out if we're the two-thousand-year-old men, both Nick and I acknowledge that that was a long time ago; we didn't even have dentures or toupees then. We were young, we were free, and beer was cheap.

I don't bring this up because I'm desperate to relive my youth. A full head of hair would be nice, but I'd rather not go back to sleeping on a futon, thank you very much. I bring it up because the book that you now hold in your hands actually started then.

That's when I first saw the talent, skills, and insights that would—over thirty years—be tested, applied, refined, and developed to the point that they're not only worthy of being shared in book form, but that it also would be a shame if they weren't.

Before his profession was helping people with their communication challenges, Nick studied film and theatre. He was a news reporter. He got an education degree. He wrote and performed sketch comedy. Generated music. Made television appearances. Sold out live shows. Toured comedy festivals. I would call him a triple-threat talent, but if you've seen him dance, you'll understand my hesitation.

As he matured, Nick didn't abandon the arts or his performance roots. He integrated his study of and his experience in performance into the world of business. He turned the stage into a boardroom. Flipped punch lines into insights. Extended the definition of an audience to include stakeholders, colleagues, clients, and prospects. And through it all, he got standing ovations for his work.

See, Nick knows something that not many do. It's not about whether you make the pitch, deliver the speech, or give the presentation. It's about the *impact* you create. The last thing that anyone needs (other than maybe a pandemic) is another pitch. People aren't scrambling to receive another email, answer one more call, have one more Zoom meeting, or be on the receiving end of one more awkwardly worded LinkedIn connection request. No one is counting down the seconds to when they'll be pitch-slapped by someone asking, "We make apps. Do you need apps?" *Everyone* is pitching. Constantly. Now you're going to do it too?

You better be an ingenious expert because your competition isn't only the next pitch or the next speech, it's the next Instagram notification coming across your audience's personal interruption device. You better have important ideas. You better be transformative. You better be engaging. You better be clear. You better be concise. You better connect on a deeper level. You better use the art of storytelling. You better have body language that supports your message. You better have appropriate visuals. And you better have an ending they won't forget.

Sound complicated? Let me simplify it for you: you better use this book.

You have great ideas. Wonderful thoughts. Unique perspectives. Valuable products. Interesting concepts. Bold opinions.

But none of those ideas can have an impact on the world unless you communicate with impact when you present them.

Your ideas deserve it. And so do you.

RON TITE
Author of *Think. Do. Say.* and coauthor of
Everyone's an Artist (or At Least They Should Be)

INTRODUCTION

IT'S THE EARLY DAYS of the COVID-19 pandemic, and we are we are all adjusting.

My son has moved back home from university to complete his first year studying engineering virtually, and my daughter is completing her second last year of high school. Like many leaders, my wife, Helen, a senior executive who leads a large team, is working from home.

Along with what seems like everyone else on the planet, I am also working from home. I am no longer at my comfortable office and I have given my home-office workspace to my son. We are all at home, along with our two dogs, trying to live a normal life.

One month into our new reality, I find myself in our basement trying, unsuccessfully, to write a book. This book.

It isn't going well.

Write. Delete. Repeat.

Write. Delete. Repeat.

Write. Delete. Repeat.

Why am I having such a hard time? I have lots to say.

I love coaching and public speaking and communication. I also love helping people with their communication challenges, whether it's preparing for a new pitch or a custom talk or articulating a transformational strategy to engage an organization around a bold, unique vision.

I know I help people.

But fundamentally I am worried. With everything that's going on—businesses shutting their doors, recession looming, mass unemployment inevitable—people are scared, including me. I am worried that no one will require the services of a communication coach in a COVID or post-COVID world.

Shaking off the negativity, I decide to take a different approach. I am going to create a visual outline of my thinking. I am a visual thinker. To do this, I need a marker and some paper. I head upstairs from my makeshift basement office, through the kitchen and up to the second floor, down the hall and into the home office.

I open the door quietly. Helen is hosting a Microsoft Teams meeting, well into her fourth or fifth hour of meetings, even though it's only 11 a.m. She sees me and mutes herself. She motions to her screen and says, "Take a look . . ."

This is what I see.

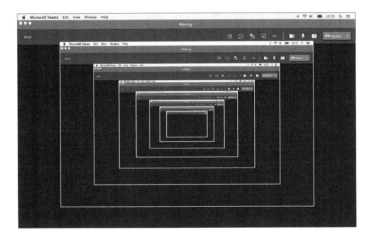

People have always taken the skill of communication for granted because they could. Or they thought they could.

It's an infinity mirror image of someone's screen. I let out a little laugh (I have an odd sense of humour), but as I do I catch Helen's eye and I realize she's not laughing. She's exasperated. She says, "It's been fifteen minutes and we still haven't started the meeting."

I smile and squeeze her shoulder with encouragement. I grab the marker and paper and make my way back to my work dungeon.

The next morning, I am out for a run with two friends, Mary and Susan. Both lead sizeable teams for large non-profit organizations. I share Helen's experience about the never-ending infinity windows and how challenging it is for her.

And boom, off they go—venting their own frustrations about the communication challenges they are facing.

"It's not the same as being there in person."

"How can I engage my donors?"

"How do I keep my team engaged?"

"I'm on Zoom all day long and I'm not getting anything done."

"I'm exhausted and so is my team."

And that's when it hits me: my work has always been important, but now it is vital. People have always taken the skill of communication for granted because they could. Or they thought they could.

You learn to walk naturally. For the most part, you learn to talk naturally too. And for many, "winging it" when speaking in public is par for the course. But here's the hard truth: winging it rarely works in your favour or your audience's favour.

Online communication is even more challenging, and we have to make an effort—a real, consistent effort—to ensure our ideas are understood.

Online communication is harder because we often can't read facial expressions or see body language to pick up cues. We often aren't close enough to leaders or comfortable enough to ask them quick clarifying questions to ensure we are moving forward in the right direction. We don't have impromptu opportunities for connection.

So yes, it's getting much more difficult to communicate. And our work lives, the way we spend the majority of our time, can become a source of frustration.

Let's up the stakes a bit, shall we? What if it's not a team of project managers or fundraising associates we are trying to connect with? What if you're a doctor connecting with a patient who is awaiting the results of a skin cancer biopsy? The doctor speaks and the patient listens—then hangs up unsure of their diagnosis and treatment options. Layer the anxiety and emotion of the listener onto the complexity and expertise of the specialist and, more often than not, you get a disconnect.

PATIENT: So you've got my results?

SPECIALIST: Yes. Your biopsy results are all positive.

PATIENT: That's good, right?

SPECIALIST: Unfortunately not. In the mass we found a malignant neoplasm.

At this point, all the patient hears are the words "mass" and "malignant." They are confused, with more questions than answers. This is more common than you might think. Pre-COVID, according to the Institute for Healthcare Communication in the United States, "less than half of hospitalized patients could identify their diagnoses or the names of their medication(s) at discharge, an indication of ineffective communication with their physicians."[1]

Why is it so hard to communicate clearly?

1 **The tools**

2 **The content**

According to a study published in the *Journal of Clinical Oncology*, only 5 percent of cancer patients with less than six months to live had an accurate understanding of their illness. Thirty-eight percent couldn't remember ever talking to their doctor about their life expectancy.[2]

Why is it so hard to communicate clearly? There are two key reasons: the tools and the content.

The exponential growth of communication technology has made our world smaller and more challenging to navigate. We have more tools and technology than ever to help us communicate: Google, Facebook, LinkedIn, Slack, Skype, Yammer, Zoom, and the list goes on.

Oh yeah, and we still have telephone and in-person meetings too.

Each of these tools can be extraordinarily helpful, but the way we have layered and combined these technologies, which were designed to help us communicate, can actually make our world of work more complex and confusing.

Take the most ubiquitous communication tool of all: email. Not long ago I received an email from a good friend, sent to me and our group of friends. The subject was "Cottage in June."

I was confused. It was July 6. And we had gone to the cottage as a group not a month ago, but thirteen months ago! The email content had *nothing* to do with the cottage. Our friend was kindly sharing some information on a band we all like and had used that email thread because he wanted to distribute it to the same group.

How many times have you received email communication from a colleague that started in one thread, continued in another, and then hopped to another and another? Following the message or actions becomes very difficult. Especially when you cannot recall who sent it and you have to search for the information by subject! It can be maddening.

This is compounded by the fact that we are living in one of the most gloriously innovative eras in the history of the world. These same exponential technologies are converging to create remarkable innovations and discoveries in energy, finance, food, biology, engineering, the environment, medicine, and more. Each of these areas is experiencing unprecedented growth and breakthroughs in process, product development, and solutions. In some instances, areas of focus are combining through the use of emerging technologies, which makes the content even more complex, requiring greater expertise and specialized knowledge. There are experts trained in all of these areas, but they are not trained in how to share their knowledge or their progress.

So, we have a communication problem sweeping the world, caused in part by technology tools and in part by the sheer complexity of the content.

The message and the mode of communication are muddied.

So, Who Is This Book For?

You're in the right place if you are what I call an *ingenious expert*. Don't run away. You likely qualify. Let me explain what I mean.

An expert is a person who has comprehensive and authoritative knowledge of or skill in a particular subject. Experts are scientists, academics, technologists, entrepreneurs, or business leaders steeped in a specific area of focus. That's the *expert* part.

You're *ingenious* if you are clever, or even try to be. You want to offer new concepts and original ideas or are working to invent something that will move your area of expertise forward.

This book
is for **the
ingenious
expert.**

Ingenious experts are everywhere. They are ophthalmologists like Dr. David Hunter at Boston Children's Hospital, who works tirelessly to change the status quo that leaves half of the children with amblyopia, a vision development disorder, undiagnosed and untreated—so he invented the blinq™ vision scanner.

You don't have to be a scientist to be an ingenious expert. You could be like Floyd Marinescu, CEO of C4 Media, who created a non-profit to promote the adoption of basic income, a cash payment unconditionally delivered to all citizens without any means testing or work requirement. Floyd is passionate about economics and became a self-educated expert in the area.

Or like Dr. Dan Swan, who recognized the opportunity for virtual reality in the real estate market to help companies make better investments.

Or Nick, who runs a software development company.

Or David, the photographer for some of Canada's best bands.

This book is for you if you are responsible for developing new technologies or software solutions or if you are responsible for teams of people who are developing new technologies or software solutions, and you need to communicate.

If you are an expert or an emerging expert in a complex area, be it science or finance or insurance, and you need to share your knowledge with others, this book is for you.

This book is also for those of you who regularly promote your business, organization, association, or product through public speaking, or if you have teams who do this and you want to improve the clarity of message delivery.

Who Is Nick Kindler?

As a trained actor, writer, comedian, and teacher, I have spent my career at the intersection of the creative and the objective. I fully explored my creative side as a comedian, writing and performing sketches on television and on stages around North America. As the owner and creative director at a mid-sized communications and events agency, I focused on the strategic objectives and outcomes required for results, and I designed and produced experiences and programs based on these desired outcomes.

For the first half of my career, I did some great work and there is a great deal I am proud of. But then came my biggest failure. It turned into my biggest win.

Over three years, post-recession, I have seen my once-successful communications and events business slowly crumble. At its peak, we were one of the "hot" agencies doing millions in revenue. By 2011, I was at a lawyer's office signing papers to dissolve my company. The reality was that I was miserable then, but I had also been miserable before the decline. The collapse of my business mirrored my diminishing interest in the actual work. My heart wasn't in it anymore.

I didn't know it then, but this was one of the best things that could have happened to me. I learned that the thing I loved the most about my business—where my heart lies and what I was exceptional at—was helping people communicate and present more effectively. I was very good at presenting and pitching. And my team was too. My clients saw this and would ask for my help. I had been providing this service, probably the most valuable and profitable service in my business, to my clients *free of charge*.

After my communication and events company closed its doors, I was starting anew and decided to focus on refining the coaching service, so I could help leaders become better communicators.

I dove in pretty quickly by giving my time away. I volunteered at the United Way to help a friend and colleague shape their Millennial Speakers' Bureau. I also volunteered for TEDxToronto as a coach, eventually becoming the head of programming. I opened my coaching consultancy, Kindler and Company, with a clear purpose: help leaders communicate with clarity and purpose so they can engage others and create meaningful change.

And an interesting thing happened. I made more personal income in my first year than I had ever made in my years working at my own agency. And others were attracted to the work.

I partnered with Singularity University and became a curation and coaching partner for its Canadian operations, and I eventually became a certifying partner for Singularity University Global. I travelled globally to help the world's deepest thinkers and smartest brains become better speakers, communicators, and educators.

In doing so, I refined and formalized my Communicate with Impact methodology. Communicate with Impact incorporates my years of experience, my time coaching and working with agency clients, TEDxToronto, Singularity University, and the hundreds of ingenious experts I have had the privilege of collaborating with and coaching. All of these ingenious experts wanted the same thing: to communicate more clearly so they can have a greater impact on their audience.

What You're Going to Learn

This book follows the same structure as my Communicate with Impact program. As you move through the three sections—Simplify, Transform, and Perform—you will learn key concepts and techniques that are easy to apply. In fact, I have made it even easier for you. At the end of each chapter, I provide you with an assignment—specific actions to take so you can prepare a talk from the germ of an idea to performance.

In the first chapter, I will share the Path to Impact, the principles by which leaders can create clarity, understanding, engagement, and impact through simplification, transformation, and performance. It's the philosophy of the program and everything that follows is based on this model.

I then make a case for why your ideas are important. Ingenious experts are change-makers—they want to change the world and can only do that if they share their knowledge. I will discuss why your idea is just as important as anyone else's in Chapter 2.

In Chapter 3, I provide you with your first tool, the Communication Canvas, which many of my clients swear by, asking me to send them a blank Communication Canvas when they have a presentation coming up.

Continuing to explore the importance of clearly structured communication, in Chapter 4 I look at how to create an ending your listeners will remember.

Many of my clients, and likely many readers of this book, are scientifically minded, and in Chapter 5, I share the neuroscience behind storytelling so you can feel comfortable and confident using these tools and techniques.

In Chapter 6, I reveal an incredibly versatile storytelling tool to help you create and share your stories called the Story Spine. The Story Spine is so easy to use and so accessible that you may never tell another story again without it.

The goal of this book is to help you communicate with impact. Of course, language plays a significant role in communication, so in Chapter 7 we explore rhetorical devices and emotional language that will help you connect with your audience in a deeper way.

In Chapter 8, we then revisit the Communication Canvas and examine how to integrate story and rhetoric within the framework of your talk. By this point, if you are following along, you will have developed a draft of your talk.

Once you have a talk that's clear, concise, and incorporates story and emotional language, we dive into the stagecraft of presenting. Chapter 9 explores how to set the stage for a successful delivery by establishing your space with the right lighting, sound, and environment.

As an ingenious expert, what visuals are you going to use to display your content to your audience? In Chapter 10, we discuss the role of visuals to enhance (and not distract from) your talk, and I provide five questions to help you determine whether or not your slides are worthy of presentation.

In Chapter 11, I walk you through the universality of performance. That's right: no matter who you are or what you do, you're a performer. I show you how to claim your space and shape your performance in any setting (including online). I also share the physical characteristics of status, which can help you show up the way you want to be seen.

There is a "fear factor" that kicks in whenever you present, no matter who you are, and it changes how we communicate with our bodies. In Chapter 12, we uncover how to use body language and gestures to communicate without words.

Then, in Chapter 13, we move into your head as I share the one key facial expression that you need to use every time you present. I show you how to embrace the Three Levers of Voice to help you connect with your audience.

So, what are you waiting for? Get ready to communicate with impact.

In Chapter 14, we bring it all together by exploring rehearsal techniques that will ensure you remember your talk and help you deliver time and again.

Finally, in the Conclusion, I wrap things up with a plea to you, dear ingenious expert. I ask you to consider the tool of communication as a gift that can be shared to help make the world a better place.

So, what are you waiting for? Get ready to simplify, transform, and perform. Get ready to communicate with impact.

PART 1

SIMPLIFY

SIMPLIFY

SIMPLIFY

SIMPLIFY

SIMPLIFY

SIMPLIFY

SIMPLIFY

1

THE PATH TO IMPACT

NOT LONG AGO I was coaching a young regenerative research scientist named Laura, helping her develop a talk based on her findings. Laura, like many regenerative scientists, was focused on a tiny little problem: developing a cure for diabetes.

We were stuck. I was having a hard time getting her to articulate the purpose of her talk. She kept telling me, passionately, about specific readings and measurements, which, as I am not a regenerative scientist, didn't mean much to me. When I asked her to explain the purpose behind the readings and measurements, it made even less sense.

We had a limited number of sessions and I wanted to get some traction. So, I decided to change things up. I asked her, "Tell me about your workday. What happens from the moment you wake up to the moment you close your eyes?"

She told me that after she finishes her morning routine of exercise, breakfast, and so on, she arrives at her lab at around 7:30 and checks "the readings and measurements to ensure that nothing has changed overnight and that the regenerated pancreas..."

"Sorry, can you repeat that last part?" I wanted to make sure I hadn't misheard.

"I check the readings and measurements to ensure that nothing has changed overnight and that the regenerated pancreas . . ."

Smiling, I asked her, "Are you saying that you have actually regenerated a pancreas?"

"Yes." She looked at me like I was joking.

"I didn't know that was possible."

"Oh yes, sure it is. That has been happening for a while now," she said smiling. "The challenge isn't regenerating the pancreas; it's vascularizing the body so the pancreas will be accepted and work within the body successfully. That's what I am working on."

And just like that—a breakthrough! For Laura and me, at least. Her work continues.

This is where we focused. Because if Laura and her team can successfully vascularize a pancreas, the part of the body that produces insulin, she can help find a cure for diabetes, which caused 1.5 million deaths in 2019.[1] Laura's work is important. She just didn't know how to express herself.

I would argue that your work is important too. Replace regenerative scientist with your job title: financial advisor or environmental response coordinator or dermatologist or ophthalmologist or information systems director. The world of work, no matter what you do, has become more and more complex. Do you understand the impact your work can have on the world? Do your teams, your clients, and your community? Do they even understand what you do?

Although many of us have heard of blockchain, most of us don't truly understand what it is. And while we all have heard of regenerative medicine, did you know that we can *actually* regenerate a pancreas?

When I ask this question in my talks and workshops, 90 percent of people say they had no idea this kind of innovation had become a reality. And that's a shame, because we are *very* close to solving some of the world's biggest problems. We should know this.

I think it's fair to say that we all, regardless of our job title, want to have an impact in our work, in our community, in our home. And we can. But we need to be able to wade through the complexities of our work and the supportive technologies in order to *communicate* clearly.

The good news is that this is possible. There is a model that will help you, your math genius neighbour, or your rocket scientist/socialite friend communicate with impact.

I call it the Path to Impact.

THE PATH TO IMPACT

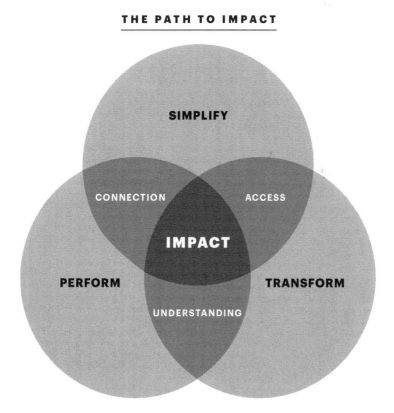

Be bold.
Unlearn.
Share.
Focus.
Have fun.

As leaders we must *simplify* our messaging so it's accessible. Then we must *transform* the message. Take the communication in its simplified form and transform it so your audience can understand it and relate to it. And from there, we take our transformed content and *perform* it with confidence and style so we can connect and engage with others.

If we *simplify*, we will provide access to those who normally would not be exposed to the content. If we *transform*, we will help people understand. If we *perform*, we will create engagement. In doing so, we will have a real *impact*.

It's more than just a pretty picture. The Path to Impact model works. It has been embraced by scientists and speakers and educators and entrepreneurs and business leaders from Amsterdam to Toronto and from Brazil to Italy, from blockchain experts to those seeking economic reform. The model helps them clarify their message and engage powerfully with their audience.

This book operates as a handbook of sorts. If you follow the simple instructions, answer the questions, and do the work, you will complete a comprehensive, original, well-developed, and well-delivered talk. So, as you dive into this book, I ask you to remember that this is a process that is tried and tested. A process that works.

When I am delivering this method as part of one of my programs, I ask all attendees to agree to some basic rules of engagement. And as I am only here to prompt you along in the written word, I would like to share these rules with you too.

1   Be bold. You are going to generate ideas as you read this book and you are going to need to share them. And that can be scary. Don't hold back. Step forward with your big ideas, no matter how outlandish they may seem. This requires you to challenge yourself to get it done—*no matter what*.

2 Unlearn. Unlearning means removing barriers to new concepts, new ideas, and new opportunities without judgment. I may share ideas here that seem counterintuitive or may be contradictory to something you have been taught. That's okay. Please take the old piece of knowledge and metaphorically remove it from your brain. You can pick it up later. But I want you to create space for new learning.

3 Share. You will need to share your bold ideas throughout this process. I truly believe that ideas, all ideas, are worth sharing. Make sure you are ready to offer them to people you trust.

4 Focus. As I write this, I have a timer counting down. I have blocked all notifications and silenced my phone. I have told my family I am not to be disturbed and I am listening to Glenn Gould's *Bach: The Goldberg Variations* (my writing music). I have dedicated time to getting my thoughts on paper (digitally!). As you read through this book and develop your own talk, eliminate the "weapons of mass distraction"—phones, tablets, computers, and all their notifications and reminders—and give yourself the gift of protected time and space to develop your thinking and ideas.

5 Have fun. It's supposed to be fun! It may feel daunting. Overwhelming, even. But my goal is to break down the process of developing a talk or a presentation in a way that is fun, maybe even a little entertaining.

We've all had the experience where an excellent teacher or boss or friend explains something to us so well, so clearly, and so memorably that we recall not just the content but the environment and the experience of the learning. That's communicating with impact.

A journey of a thousand miles begins with the step of simplicity.

When we communicate clearly and concisely, when our words have impact, it feels good! We know we have reached others. We have helped people. We have helped shape the world. Communication can truly make the world a better place. And so can you.

I hope you'll join me on this journey to help make the world a better place by improving how we communicate.

There is a Chinese proverb which states, "A journey of a thousand miles begins with a single step." I will politely paraphrase and say, "A journey of a thousand miles begins with the step of simplicity."

HOMEWORK

1   Choose a date for your talk. Even if it means you're sharing
    it with your neighbour over dinner, draw a line in the sand to
    help you move forward. Write it down on your calendar.

2   Next, in order to motivate you to follow through, choose
    a consequence for yourself that makes you *really* uncom-
    fortable. For me, when I was writing this book, I decided
    it would be a donation to a political group to which I was
    ideologically opposed. The idea of helping fund them made
    my stomach churn. You could go bigger or more public.
    Running down the street in your underwear. Eating a jar of
    pickles. Choose something you would like to avoid at all
    costs. Whatever makes you squirm!

3   Choose a title for your talk. Yes, a title. It may sound
    premature, but don't worry, you can always change it later.
    Choose a title that sounds intriguing and compelling. Write
    a number of different options down, up to ten. Circle
    your favourite.

2

YOUR IDEA MATTERS

IDEAS ARE LIKE RIVERS. They start as a trickle somewhere far off. High up on a mountaintop, ice and snow melt and join that trickle and it slowly builds and flows down, down, down. Slowly but surely the waters come together and move from way out there into the world until they finally get to you.

Your idea is starting somewhere far off, high up within you. Perhaps it's tucked away in the recesses of your mind. Perhaps it's in a file folder or a notebook or an email on your phone. Or perhaps it's on a cocktail napkin in the glovebox of your car. It's there. It's waiting.

Here's the thing: if you have an idea that you think has potential and you *don't* share it with the world . . . well, shame on you! Ideas have tremendous power and potential. Steven Spielberg once said, "All good ideas start out as bad ideas, that's why it takes so long." Although he didn't write many of his blockbuster movies, imagine a world without *E.T.* or *Jaws* because Spielberg decided "Nah, a big shark is too silly," or "An alien that befriends a kid is stupid."

Let's take it further. Imagine a world where *no* ideas get shared. Nothing.

This is a world of stasis. Where innovation and change and creativity don't exist. A world where penicillin was

Ideas are the **lifeblood of innovation.**

never invented. A world where the *Mona Lisa* was never painted. Where the musical *Hamilton* was never produced. Where Queen's "Bohemian Rhapsody" never hit the airwaves. All because those brilliant creators kept their ideas to themselves.

Ideas are the lifeblood of innovation. They require risk, collaboration, and flexibility, as well as a dose of both humility and conceit.

Not long ago, I was working with a brilliant leader in the area of energy. Jane Kearns is the VP of growth services at MaRS Discovery District, one of the world's foremost accelerators and incubators for innovation. Jane has helped dozens of companies in the energy sector move from business idea to successful enterprise, and in 2018 she joined me at one of my speaking intensives designed to take leaders from idea to polished talk in a few very busy days. She was there to learn how to become a better speaker and she thought she might be able to share her learnings with the companies she mentors.

At dinner after the first day, I told her I thought she had a tremendous amount to offer the world as a speaker on renewable energy. She laughed and replied glibly, "I am not the one you would want for that. But thanks." She then recommended another well-known speaker. Let's call him "John."

I told her I knew who John was (an excellent speaker and one of the foremost experts on renewable energy) and had seen him speak, but I knew she could be like John, only better. "I think you're selling yourself short."

Jane smiled and said, "Well, I mean, I am not really an expert. I mean, John is *the* expert."

I politely asked her to tell me about her experience in the energy sector. She could see where this was going, but she went along with it. She told me about her years spent as a venture capitalist in New York. She talked about her time in the energy industry working with some of the most leading-edge companies in the world and how she had helped them articulate their value and grow. As she spoke, she could easily explain not just the complicated technology the company had invented but also the complex environmental problem it solved. Within a few minutes, she had outlined a massive amount of content that would provide incredible value to audiences around the world.

I pointed this out and said, "You are right. You are not John. You are different. You are better."

A few months later, Jane became a faculty member at SingularityU Canada and began speaking around the globe to business leaders about exponential technologies and the future of energy technology.

Many of us are like Jane. We are afraid of putting ourselves out there. As Marianne Williamson wrote in *A Return to Love*, "Our deepest fear is not that we are inadequate. Our deepest fear is that we are powerful beyond measure. It is our light, not our darkness, that most frightens us."[1]

We think, "It's not good enough. It doesn't make sense. I am not smart enough. No one will listen to me."

These thoughts are dangerous. They kill innovation and opportunity. So, let's do the following: let's recognize these thoughts, welcome them to the meeting, and then keep them in a separate breakout room . . . indefinitely. Your small ideas must be shared so they can transform from a trickle into a current and from a current into a wave. A wave that can change the world.

My friend and client Floyd Marinescu started a wave. As I mentioned in the Introduction, he's a successful CEO running C4 Media, which offers content and education conferences for software development gurus. Floyd was already extraordinarily successful when I met him five years ago, but he was frustrated. He saw the proliferation of AI and automation,

Your ideas are **worth sharing.**

which was helping him grow his business and become wealthy, but it was also exacerbating a massive income gap in society. Floyd had come from a working-class family with limited means and had seen the impact of globalization and automation on his father, a tool and die machinist who had lost his job in the 1980s.

Floyd wanted to speak about his big idea: basic income. Basic income provides all members of society with a low level of income so we can operate with freedom to develop, build, or work without the constraints of keeping the lights on. The fundamentals of food and board are covered by society. It wasn't a new idea, but Floyd was passionate about it. He also worried, "Who am I to share this message?"

I asked, "If not you, then who?"

I worked with Floyd for about two years. I helped him develop several different talks. He spoke at libraries full of concerned citizens, he met with politicians, he spoke on TV, and he delivered a successful TEDx Talk. Over those two years, he spoke dozens of times and started a CEOs for Basic Income group, proving that this was an idea that could be embraced by those worried about the health of capitalism. Politicians reach out to him, and quote him, regularly. He has become a recognized thought leader on basic income.

Like Floyd's ideas, your ideas matter. Your ideas are worth sharing. Your ideas cannot just change *your* world: your ideas can change *everyone's* world.

If not you, then who?

Now we've gotten that out of the way, let's talk about how to articulate your ideas in a way that is simple and understandable. In the next chapter, I share with you the secret to simplicity that will help you not just in your talks, presentations, and pitches but in *all* your communications.

HOMEWORK

1 If you haven't marked your calendar for the delivery date, do it now. If you have, take a look at the date and remind yourself of the consequences you have chosen if you do *not* deliver.

2 Are you happy with the title of your talk? If so, share it with a few trusted friends. Send them an email saying, "I am working on my next talk for [insert audience] to be delivered [insert date] and I have tentatively called it '[insert title].' I would love to get your thoughts! What do you think?"

3

THE
SECRET OF
STRUCTURE

I PROMISED YOU THE SECRET, and I won't keep you waiting, so here it is. The secret to simplifying communication is structure.

Of course, we all know innately how vital structure is. It's why education is segmented into courses or a syllabus, and courses into lessons. It's why new buildings are first conceived as drawings and project plans. And it is why pilots have a step-by-step process to take a plane from ground to air and back to ground again, all written in a handbook and guided along by air traffic control.

We also use structure to simplify our daily lives. Many of us use day planners, to-do lists, tabs, Post-it Notes. There is a billion-dollar app industry built on helping us simplify our days and stay organized.

And then there's your closet. The closet is the ultimate structural simplification system. Think about it. When you get yourself ready in the morning, you don't go to a big pile of clothes you keep on the floor looking for underwear, pants, shirt, belt . . . Where are those socks? Nope, not those . . . Where are they?! No, you go to your closet with its clear, simple structure: The shirt is on a hanger. The pants are too. Socks are in the sock drawer. You get the picture.

We know that when we simplify any complex product, process, or system, it becomes much easier to share with others so they can understand it or use it.

And yet when it comes to our communication, we rarely do this. Like a dishwasher, like a closet, we need a tool to help us guide our thinking and simplify our approach, so we can help people understand what we want them to take away.

Allow me to introduce you to the dishwasher of presentations, the closet of talks, a structure that you can use anytime, anywhere, to help you develop your ideas from scratch and provide simplicity, clarity, and understanding: the Communication Canvas. You can download a free version of it from my website, impactbook.ca/tools.

First, I am going to walk you through the Communication Canvas in the way you would use it to *deliver* a talk. Then I am going to walk you through the Communication Canvas in the way you would use it to *develop* that talk. Because they are very different.

Delivering a Talk

For many, delivering a talk goes something like this:

INTRODUCTION: You share your credentials and introduce your topic.

MIDDLE: You dive in and share the bulk of your content, perhaps supported by some statistics and facts.

CLOSE: You move abruptly to close the talk, sometimes this is signalled with "I am going close now," and you share an unclear call to action.

And here is the Communication Canvas:

COMMUNICATION CANVAS

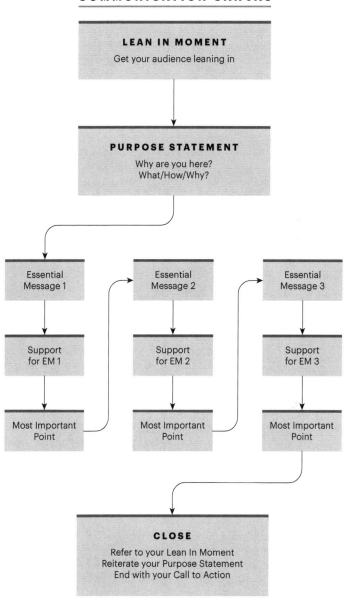

LEAN IN MOMENT
Get your audience leaning in

PURPOSE STATEMENT
Why are you here?
What/How/Why?

Essential Message 1

Essential Message 2

Essential Message 3

Support for EM 1

Support for EM 2

Support for EM 3

Most Important Point

Most Important Point

Most Important Point

CLOSE
Refer to your Lean In Moment
Reiterate your Purpose Statement
End with your Call to Action

The Purpose Statement is the most important part of your presentation or talk. **The Purpose Statement is** the most important part of your presentation or talk. The Purpose Statement is **the most important part of** your presentation or talk. The Purpose Statement is the most important part of **your presentation or talk.** The Purpose Statement is the most important part of your presentation or talk.

Lean In Moment

Think about the best talks or presentations you've ever seen. Although very different in nature, delivery, idea, or even tone, they all likely had a big moment that commanded your attention right from the beginning.

I call this the Lean In Moment. A good Lean In Moment is built around a story. (In Chapters 5 and 6 we explore the unique power of story on the human brain and how to craft a story using the Story Spine, so sit tight.) The Lean In Moment captures the audience's attention. It is often story based, but it can also be a great joke. Humour is always welcome. The story can even incorporate a few shocking statistics or a surprising fact.

What kind of story should you share here? Find a story that works for you, that you are comfortable sharing, and, most important, that connects with your Purpose Statement. The best stories are ones that belong to the storyteller. They come from your experiences, your past. Every one of us has rich details of our life to draw upon. Conversely, you can be passionate about a story you've read about or a unique historical moment that you've researched, but you need to *love* it. You really do. And, as I have already mentioned, it needs to connect with your purpose.

Purpose Statement

The Purpose Statement is the most important part of your presentation or talk.

And here's why: everything you do within your talk or presentation will depend on the clarity of this statement. It is your argument, proposal, proposition, and thesis all rolled into one. Because it is so important, it is something you should devote time to perfecting. When I work with TED or Singularity University speakers, we can spend two or sometimes three hour-long sessions developing the right Purpose Statement. Because their ideas are extraordinarily complex and sometimes not yet fully baked, it can be challenging. We need to simplify. Time to bring out a structure!

Three Step Purpose Practice

Welcome to the Purpose Practice, a process within the Communication Canvas to help determine your Purpose Statement, the statement upon which your entire presentation is based.

Step 1: Choose Your Talk

The first question is, what kind of presentation are you building? You really only have six options. Your presentation will do one of these things:

- **INFORM:** This kind of presentation provides the audience with an update or shares new information or knowledge. It's usually focused on facts and is brief.

- **EDUCATE:** This kind of presentation helps the audience build a new understanding. The more complex the content, the more time needed in a presentation to help the audience learn it.

- **PERSUADE:** Think of this as the debate model of presentations. The presenter argues for an approach or method to convince the audience to use it. A persuasive presentation is most often used in sales.

- **ACTIVATE:** This type of presentation helps an audience to start doing something new or take a decisive course of action.

- **INSPIRE:** The speaker strives to engage the hearts and minds of the audience in this kind of presentation. The goal is to move them to think differently, act differently, or change their behaviour in a fundamental way.

- **ENTERTAIN:** In these presentations, the goal is to amuse the audience and create an enjoyable experience. The more enjoyable, the more they will remember the speaker and the content.

Yes, you can have elements of Inspiration in an Education talk or Entertainment in an Activation talk. Make it your own. But first you must ask yourself, "Overall, what kind of presentation am I building? Why am I here?"

Don't get hung up on this. Just choose the one that makes the most sense.

Step 2: Craft Your Purpose

Next, the Purpose Practice requires you to ask three questions:

- **WHAT?** What is my talk about? What is the subject? What is the topic? Ideally this is articulated in a word or two.

- **HOW?** What action will be taken around the topic or subject? This often has verbs and moves the topic forward in a unique way.

- **WHY?** What is the future state you will create with that action? What does it look like? What is the potential?

The Purpose Practice may seem easy, but getting it right can be challenging.

I worked with John, a brilliant ophthalmologist in the Bahamas who was a closet part-time economist. In fact, economics was his passion. He was working with policy makers, leaders, and academics to reimagine the world's economic system, *and* running a full-time practice. This is no small feat! He had come up with an idea that could revolutionize how our banking system, how our global economy, operates.

When we started our first session, I walked him through the fundamentals of the methodology, and then I asked him, "What is the purpose of your talk?"

As he spoke, he shared a lot of information about people requiring knowledge about how our economy and banking system operates. How once they have that knowledge, they can take appropriate actions. He went into great detail about the origins of the current financial system and spoke about how the monetary system was controlled by the banks and how currencies lose trillions of dollars of value every year. And how he was working with a group at the University of Toronto to build a new currency that was developed with artificial intelligence and built on the gold standard and . . .

I had heard a lot of very interesting information, but we were running out of time. So I politely interrupted him (this happens with a lot of my clients) and we dove into the Purpose Practice.

First, we tackled step 1 and agreed that John's talk was majoring in Persuasion with a minor in Education. After three one-hour sessions, we got to this:

WHAT? A new digital currency.

HOW? Used by anyone, anywhere, anytime, and will always hold value, serving the needs of every global citizen.

WHY? Has the potential to create a world of prosperity and wealth.

Step 3: Articulate Your Purpose

Once you have your What/How/Why, it's time to mould those pieces into a well-crafted Purpose Statement by generating a first draft using Language Lures and then refining it, or as I like to call it, Iterate and Edit.

I introduced John to Language Lures. Language Lures are ways to connect seemingly disparate sentences and help them flow into a Purpose Statement.

WHAT? Today I want to talk to you about [subject].

HOW? And how/Because/That can be

WHY? So that/And

By using Language Lures, you can piece your ideas together in a rough statement. I have taken John's What/How/Why and used Language Lures as connectors:

Today I want to talk to you about a new digital currency *that can be* used by anyone, anywhere, anytime *and* has the potential to create a world of prosperity and wealth.

Great! You have a draft of a Purpose Statement. But you're not done yet! The next component of the final step of the Purpose Practice is to Iterate and Edit. This is your opportunity to remove the Language Lures, cut the copy down, revise, and ensure you love it.

Here is where John landed:

There is a new digital currency that is highly accessible, always holds value, and has the potential to create a world of prosperity and wealth.

Boom! A Purpose Statement!

Three Step Purpose Practice

1 **Choose your talk**

2 **Craft your purpose**

3 **Articulate your purpose**

When I finished working with John, he paused and smiled and said, "Wow! This is great, man. This is so helpful!" A few weeks later he shared that he had used the Purpose Practice and Communication Canvas to prepare for another important meeting. He said, "I used it just like you showed me and my client said, 'I have never heard anything so complex explained so clearly.'" Then he smiled and, with a big laugh, said, "Go, Nick, go!" It made my day.

Now that we've got the Purpose Statement underway, let's move on and explore the rest of the Communication Canvas.

Essential Messages

Essential Messages are the basic support for your structure. If the Communication Canvas represents a closet, then your Essential Messages are hangers. Hangers of information. Hangers of statistics. Hangers of stories.

Here's the good news: unlike the Purpose Statement, which can be challenging to distill and develop, Essential Messages are often based on the stuff you already know. If you take the time to be very clear in defining your Purpose Statement, then your Essential Messages will be much easier to identify and articulate.

Like building an argument, each Essential Message serves to support your Purpose Statement. If you are absolutely certain that your Purpose Statement is perfect, then it will not need any modification no matter what your Essential Messages are. But as you develop your Essential Messages, you may begin to question if your Purpose Statement is right. This can be frustrating, but it's awesome! It's an opportunity for you to kick the tires and ask, "Does this work?" These messages are going to take you, and eventually your audience, on a journey, and if the tire pressure is too low, then you'll find yourself stuck on the side of the road.

Let's look at how John did. Recall that his Purpose Statement was "There is a new digital currency that is highly accessible, always holds value, and has the potential to create a world of prosperity and wealth."

After sifting through a lot of material, we landed on these three messages, as each one reinforces his Purpose Statement:

1 Why we need a new digital currency.
2 The new currency must be people-centric.
3 Introducing the new currency will change the shape of the global economy.

Essential Message 1, "Why we need a new digital currency," addresses the unasked question in the Purpose Statement: "If you're introducing me to a new currency, then what is wrong with the old one?" It also helps lay the groundwork and explain why currency is built the way it is.

Essential Message 2, "Must be people-centric," addresses the need for the currency to be "highly accessible and always holding value." Both are about the user of the currency and are a dramatic shift from how other currencies are developed and managed.

Essential Message 3, "Introducing the new currency," lifts the curtain on how this new currency will be created, but more importantly it illustrates the impact it can have on the world. This part of the talk highlights how the currency "has the potential to create a world of prosperity and wealth."

Each Essential Message answers or addresses items implied or mentioned in the Purpose Statement.

Support for Essential Messages

Now comes the even easier part. Once you have three Essential Messages that reinforce your Purpose Statement, you can fill in the important information to drive that information home. Remember all the incredible, vast amount of knowledge John shared with me when I initially asked him the purpose of his talk? This is where that information gets placed.

If we are sticking with the closet analogy, it should now be easy to place this information on the appropriate hanger. The Support for Essential Messages 1, 2, and 3 are statistics, case studies, facts, and stories. Yes, even stories! Each item you add makes your foundation stronger and easier for others to understand. As you develop your draft, add it all in. All the facts. All the stats. All the stories. You will likely have to remove some later, but start by placing each one into its spot.

Here is John's draft Support for Essential Message 1: "Why we need a new digital currency."

- Present scenario: currencies lose value every year
- Government and central banks are printing trillions
- The more money they print, the less value the currency holds
- Loaves of bread analogy
- The monetary system is controlled by the banks and not by the people

You can see that John is adding facts ("Currencies lose value every year"; "Government and central banks are printing trillions") and he is also planning to share a story via an analogy ("Loaves of bread"). Analogy is a very helpful translation tool for complex ideas (more on this in Chapter 4).

How many Essential Messages and Supports do you need? It really depends. You can do a great five- to ten-minute talk with only one Essential Message and Support. But the Lean In

Moment, Essential Message, and Support need to be robust. Like any good structure, there is strength in threes. So, having three Essential Messages is perfect for a fifteen- to twenty-minute talk.

The general rule is get down all your ideas for Essential Messages and Supports, and if you have to edit, adjust, or even remove one of the messages, then so be it. A better problem than not having enough to say!

Most Important Point

Thcrc is an old saying in the marketing communications industry: Tell 'em. Tell 'em again. Then tell 'em what you told 'em.

This mantra comes into play a few times throughout the Communication Canvas, which is why I recommend reiterating one of your Essential Messages. It may seem odd. I mean, you will have just shared it a few minutes ago. But if you want people to remember your content, you need to reiterate. I don't mean repeat the exact same words. I mean share the same message in a slightly different way. This is one easy way for you to ensure your communication has impact.

Conclusion

After you develop your final Most Important Point, it's time to start winding down. But don't get too excited. You're not done. Far from it!

In your Close, first you need to reiterate your Purpose Statement. Then you need to reinforce your Call to Action. What do you want your audience to do?

Be specific. Do you want them to start using a new system? Do you want them to follow a new process? Do you want them to think in a different way every time they start a project?

Tell 'em. Tell 'em. Tell 'em.
Tell 'em. Tell 'em. Tell 'em.
Tell 'em. Tell 'em. Tell 'em.
Tell 'em. Tell 'em. Tell 'em.
Tell 'em. Tell 'em. Tell 'em.
Tell 'em. Tell 'em. Tell 'em.

TELL 'EM AGAIN

Tell 'em. Tell 'em. Tell 'em.
Tell 'em. Tell 'em. Tell 'em.
Tell 'em. Tell 'em. Tell 'em.
Tell 'em. Tell 'em. Tell 'em.
Tell 'em. Tell 'em. Tell 'em.
Tell 'em. Tell 'em. Tell 'em.

You should also attempt to reconnect or refer back to your Lean In Moment. In some speeches, the Lean In Moment starts as a story and continues throughout the talk, being used to illustrate support for Essential Messages and then reaching a satisfying conclusion at the end of the talk.

Tip: Avoid the sandwich! One thing I recommend you *don't* do is create a story sandwich. You definitely want to use storytelling in your Lean In Moment, and don't forget to use it throughout your talk. It can seem jarring to an audience if you start with a story, then move into content, and then jump back into the story or a new story at the very end. You want the audience to be with you, not looking at you like they are lost.

Remember

> **PURPOSE STATEMENT**
> Why are you here?
> What/How/Why?

WHAT? What is my talk about? What is the subject? What is the topic? Ideally this is articulated in a word or two.

HOW? What action will be taken around the topic or subject? This often has verbs and moves the topic forward in a unique way.

WHY? What is the future state you will create with that action? What does it look like? What is the potential?

HOMEWORK

1 Download the Communication Canvas worksheet at impactbook.ca/tools.

2 Decide from the six options which kind of presentation you are developing.

3 Choose your What—what is your talk's subject?

4 Choose your How—the action that will be taken around the topic or subject.

5 Choose your Why—the future state you will create with that action.

6 Piece together your What/How/Why with Language Lures to build your Purpose Statement.

7 Iterate and Edit: cut and revise until you love it.

8 Having trouble getting motivated? Remember the date and consequence you chose. If that's not enough, then let's get you some help. I recommend finding an accountability partner. If you don't have a friend who wants to support you and be supported, there are some terrific programs to help you find someone who will. Try:

- GetMotivatedBuddies (getmotivatedbuddies.com)
- HabitShare (habitshareapp.com)
- Supporti (getsupporti.com)

4

AN ENDING TO REMEMBER

I F YOUR TALK IS GOOD, then people will want to talk about it, which means you'll get questions. Don't be afraid of this. Questions are a sign of engagement and the longer a question period, the better the talk. It's the opportunity for the audience and the speaker to exchange information.

And just like any good presentation, you need to plan out this exchange. Think in advance about what kinds of questions you may be asked. Write them down and then take the time to answer them. Put your answers down in bullet form. When you uncover a question you don't know the answer to, then wonderful! You have time to find out the answer or, even better, add the information into the messaging of your talk.

Thinking in advance about the exchange portion of your talk is a great way to ensure you're not missing any key content. It's also a solid way to generate more content for your next talk. The audience will always give you an indication about what else they want to know. They are providing you with a trail to follow to find your next talk.

Your Second Close will help you

STICK THE LANDING.

STICK **THE** LANDING.

STICK THE **LANDING.**

STICK THE LANDING.

STICK **THE** LANDING.

STICK THE **LANDING.**

STICK THE LANDING.

STICK **THE** LANDING.

STICK THE **LANDING.**

Welcome to the Second Close

Almost done. One last thing to think about. There is nothing worse than seeing someone deliver a killer talk with precision, get a standing ovation, then take a bunch of questions. And when exchange time is over, they ask, "Any more questions?" And there is a long, awkward pause.

Pause. Pause. Pause. They shuffle, wait, and then fill the void with "Ahem. Okay. Thanks." Then slowly walk off the stage. You've just lost the energy and enthusiasm that has been shared up until that point.

Welcome to your Second Close! The Second Close, which is much shorter than the first close, has you share three things:

1 Relate a micro one-minute story connected to the Purpose Statement.
2 Reiterate your Purpose Statement.
3 Reinforce your Call to Action.

Smile, pause, and thank the audience. A Second Close will ensure you deliver a solid ending and keep the audience with you for the duration of the talk. It helps you stick the landing, as they say.

A Short Story about Stories

I don't think there is anything as wonderful as watching a small child listen to a story. I remember enjoying stories as a child. In kindergarten when it was story time, I would be the first one on the story mat, legs crossed and waiting. My kids were the same. They would wait excitedly for their bedtime stories. Because I made many of them up, my daughter Sarah would prescribe the story she wanted, in detail. Tucked in with her stuffed animals, Lambie under one arm and Kitty Cat under the other, she would announce, "Tell the one about Kitty Cat and Lambie. Scary but not too scary!" And as I told my daughter the story, she would often correct me, "No, Lambie met Harold the Hedgehog. And don't forget: Harold likes to talk a lot." Even though this was obviously a tactic to prolong the bedtime routine and avoid the inevitable "Lights out," she was always indulged. I loved watching her face and the expressions of awe that showed how engaged she was in every twist and turn.

I am sure this was the case for you. It's universal. When we are young, we love being told stories and are pulled into them quickly and easily. We become transfixed by tales, as they take us away from our current reality.

And if that story was sad or scary or funny or something unique happened, we remembered it. That's why Sarah often asked for a story that was "scary but not too scary!" Like all of us, she remembers the vivid details of stories. Even if we've only heard them once.

As we grow up, it seems we outgrow the desire to be told stories. We forget about the transformational power of story-telling. It seems frivolous. Unnecessary. Unless they come from a high-paid keynote speaker or TED.com, stories become an unwelcome guest in the business meeting, the boardroom, the symposium, the university or college classroom.

In his 2020 non-fiction book *The Splendid and the Vile*, Erik Larson shares how a single story, told in the right way, changed the course of history. During World War II, Dr. Reginald Victor Jones, a scientist in the British army, found technology in the wreckage of a downed German plane that meant the Germans had developed a new way to send bombers across the English Channel. Previously, pilots could only navigate in daylight or moonlight. Through his research, he discovered the Germans were developing a new kind of radar to navigate through

Don't forget
about the
**transformational
power of
storytelling.**

darkness. This was so important that Dr. Jones was unexpectedly called to explain his discovery to Prime Minister Winston Churchill and his cabinet.

Churchill asked Dr. Jones to clarify a detail. Now this was a complex technology full of intricacies, and he was speaking to a group of non-technical specialists. As Larson puts it, "Instead of merely answering, Jones said, 'Would it help, sir, if I told you the story right from the start?'" Dr. Jones then shared his findings "as a detective story, describing the early clues and the subsequent accumulation of evidence." He revealed some fresh intelligence, including a note pulled just three days earlier from a German bomber that seemed to confirm his hunch that radio beams guided German pilots blitzing Britain. Dr. Jones used this information to counter the enemy planes by jamming "the German pilots' ears with electronic nonsense, tricking the attacking Luftwaffe into taking aim at open fields or lakes instead of cities."[1]

Without this knowledge, or the translation of this content, the whole course of the war could have shifted in a disastrous way for Britain. "He did more to save us from disaster than many who are glittering with trinkets," Winston Churchill said.[2] And all because Dr. Jones translated the complexity of his finding in a way that could be understood by others. He told a story.

Stories play a vital role in the successful development and delivery of any presentation. Now that we have walked through in detail the powerful simplifying structure of the Communication Canvas, you can see that storytelling plays a significant role not just at the beginning and ending but throughout your talk. Over the next couple of chapters, I want to help you understand *why* storytelling is such a powerful communication tool and then *how* to use it.

HOMEWORK

1 Brainstorm what questions you might be asked after your presentation. Write them all down, then try to answer them. Can any of that content be added into your talk?

2 Is there a short, one-minute story you could share as a Second Close? Don't worry about writing it just yet. Just brainstorm. Storytelling is coming up next!

PART 2

TRANSFORM

TRANSFORM

TRANSFORM

TRANSFORM

TRANSFORM

TRANSFORM

TRANSFORM

5

WHY STORY MATTERS

A NUMBER OF YEARS AGO I was working with a brilliant regenerative scientist by the name of Thin. Thin and I had started working on the Communication Canvas. After a couple of sessions, she had developed a well-structured talk on the challenge of finding the "truth and uncovering the story in your scientific data." She had gone through the entire process and was ready to develop the Lean In Moment. In short, the talk needed a story. I could tell she was uneasy about the storytelling aspect. As a scientist, she could get behind process and structure, but I was asking her to bring something seemingly unrelated to her talk. To help settle her unease, I prescribed her the task of finding a story that worked for her. Ideally, something personal.

On the day of our next session, she sat down across from me and didn't make eye contact. She was quiet and reserved. I feared that she had been unable to complete her homework, so I asked her how her quest for a story had gone. To my surprise, she said, "I think I may have found something."

She then shared with me a quote from *The Things They Carried* by Tim O'Brien, a collection of fictional but sometimes autobiographical stories of the Vietnam War. I was a little worried as I wanted her story to be personal, from her own experience. But I smiled and asked her to share it with me.

(Warning: The following quote has graphic and vivid descriptions of violence that may be disturbing.) She then recited this passage:[1]

I want you to feel what I felt. I want you to know why story-truth is truer sometimes than happening-truth. Here is the happening-truth. I was once a soldier. There were many bodies, real bodies with real faces, but I was young then and I was afraid to look. And now, twenty years later, I'm left with faceless responsibility and faceless grief. Here is the story-truth. He was a slim, dead, almost dainty young man of about twenty. He lay in the center of a red clay trail near the village of My Khe. His jaw was in his throat. His one eye was shut, the other eye was a star-shaped hole. I killed him.

I was transported back to a childlike state. I listened, my eyes wide. Not only was the writing beautiful, but it was disturbing and haunting. I was blown away. I couldn't speak for a full minute.

To fill the silence, Thin told me that her family was from Vietnam, not far from the village mentioned in the story. She had found a story and a quote that would connect with her Purpose Statement about "uncovering the story in your scientific data" and make an emotional connection with the audience. It was perfect. Using this story, she beautifully illustrated the purpose of her talk: how story can help create a deeper understanding of facts. This fundamental difference between sharing facts and sharing experience can help create a deeper level of understanding for the listener.

In addition, she introduced me to the concept of Happening-Truth and Story-Truth. I told her that this quote not only worked, but I would like her permission to share it with my speakers and students.

Sharing experience can help **create a deeper level of understanding** than sharing facts.

The Happening-Truth is a list of facts:

- I was a soldier
- There were many bodies
- I was young
- I was afraid to look
- Now I grieve

The Story-Truth focuses on the fictionalized details of the experience:

- Slim, dead, almost dainty
- One eye shut
- Star-shaped hole

As readers or listeners of this story, we will easily remember the Story-Truth, and it will help us to remember the Happening-Truth facts.

The impact of stories on the human brain is fascinating. If you're not taking advantage of the power of storytelling, you're missing out. You are not leveraging all the tools in your toolbelt.

Seven versus Two

Imagine you're running a business that has all the resources it needs. In order to deliver your products and services, you require all seven divisions running smoothly: Sales, Marketing, Operations, Administration, Finance, Human Resources, Technology. If they are, you will have the impact you want: $10 million a year! Now imagine, for some reason, you can run only two at a time. Let's say Sales and Administration. What happens? You are going to be under-delivering and underper-forming, and especially if you are the business owner, you will be frustrated and worried.

Only two is the scenario that takes place in our brains when someone shares facts alone: only two areas of the brain are activated: Wernicke's area, which focuses on language processing, and Broca's area, which focuses on language comprehension. But if you share a descriptive tale, seven areas of the brain are engaged and all kinds of incredible things start to happen.

Area of the Brain	Purpose	Message
Visual cortex	Recognizes and identifies colours and shapes	Is that a stop sign?
Olfactory cortex	Identifies scents and smells	Skunk!
Auditory cortex	Perceives and interprets sounds	I can't concentrate with all the construction noise!
Motor cortex	Controls the execution of movement	Stay away from the ledge!
Sensory cortex and cerebellum	Perceives texture through touch	That feels soft!
Wernicke's area	Responsible for the comprehension of speech	I understand what they are saying.
Broca's area	Focuses on language comprehension	I can express what I heard or what they said.

A story can help us remember. A Stanford Graduate School of Business study cited in *The Atlantic* noted that when information is woven into a narrative, people recall it "up to 22 times more than facts alone."[2] A study conducted in the 1960s found that people have different levels of information retention based on *how* information is delivered to them and that "retention is six to seven times higher through stories."[3]

In addition to Wernicke's area and Broca's area, other parts of the brain get activated with story. Each area plays a significant role in how we perceive information.

Researchers from Emory University published a study in *Brain & Language* magazine that showed that when participants in a lab measuring cortex activity were read descriptive language like, "He had rough leathery hands" or "She had a velvet singing voice," their sensory cortex activated. When the same subjects were read equivalent but non-evocative language, like "He had rough hands" or "She had a nice voice," the sensory cortex was not activated![4] A story helps us *feel*.

Since the motor and sensory areas of the brain are activated by action and sensory descriptive words, a storyteller can almost re-create his or her reality in the listener's brain by using those words. This is called *mirroring*.

Not long ago, I almost fell into a river while climbing across it. I was moving from slippery rock to slippery rock and then balancing the rest of the way on a moss-covered log. Reading this description can conjure up all kinds of reactions in the brain and may have helped you envision yourself in the story. When we immerse ourselves in learning, live in another country to learn a language, or try out a different role for a day, we are learning by experiencing something new. Mirroring does just that. A story helps us *understand*.

If we listen to a story that is suspenseful, we tense up and wonder, "What is going to happen?" It is at this point that our brains are releasing cortisol, a chemical that helps us focus. This is the same synaptic reaction that took place in our ancestors' brains when they were hunting for food or bringing down a woolly mammoth. A story helps us *focus.*

When we get to the end of a good story and it has reached a satisfying conclusion, another remarkable thing happens: our brain releases dopamine and our stress lessens. We feel happy. A story helps us *relax.*

Stories help us feel, understand, focus, relax, and, most important for our purposes, retain information. We can have all seven divisions working for us or settle on only two (with just statistics/facts) and get limited results. What would you rather have?

I know. I can sense it. Some of you are still holding out on using the tool of storytelling. And I get it. If you're a traditionally left-brained individual, a scientist or an academic, you likely don't feel comfortable embracing the tool of storytelling. When I started working with a brilliant dermatologist, Dr. Afsaneh Alavi of the Mayo Clinic, I encouraged her to share a story at the beginning of her talk. She wasn't sold. She argued, "We just don't do that in our work."

This is true. Scientific presentations are known for sharing data. But they are also known for their length. And their tedium. This doesn't have to be the case.

After I'd worked for a month with Dr. Alavi, she gave a keynote address at a scientific congress in Berlin. She is an expert in hidradenitis suppurativa (HS), a painful, long-term skin condition that causes abscesses and scarring on the skin. The exact cause of HS is unknown, but it occurs near hair follicles where there are sweat glands, usually around the groin, bottom, breasts, and armpits. This is a pretty serious subject and doesn't lend itself easily to storytelling. But Dr. Alavi shared a story at the beginning of her address.

Stories help us:

→ **feel**

→ **understand**

→ **focus**

→ **relax**

→ **retain information**

She stood confidently on stage and said, "Dreams. We all have dreams. Some of us dream of owning a bigger house. Some of us dream of winning the lottery. Some of us dream of world peace. And some of us dream ... of going on a date with George Clooney."

The silent audience erupted with laughter. She smiled and continued. "But if you have HS, you simply dream of one thing: no ... more ... pain." You could hear a pin drop.

She then went on to share a story about one of her patients who suffered from severe depression due to the pain and psychological impact of HS, and then discussed how it should be treated in a holistic way.

Dr. Alavi received rave reviews from the dermatology and surgical community and has gone on to speak at dozens and dozens of global conferences. She now understands and embraces the power of storytelling. Just because she is speaking about a serious scientific subject doesn't mean she can't tell a story. In fact, when she does tell a story, she knows she will have a *greater* impact on her audience.

During one of my speaking intensives, I witnessed a similar transformation in an experienced Canadian ophthalmologist. After experiencing the power of storytelling by seeing colleague after colleague succeed, he shared, "My next presentation will share the story of Spider-Man because, like Spider-Man, we surgeons have great power, and with great power comes great responsibility." This was how he was going to approach teaching ophthalmological fellows surgical technique. My inner nerd loved this. I was grinning from ear to ear.

The power of storytelling is not a secret. It's a tool that's been used in marketing and advertising for decades. It's even an important part of shaping products and services—experience design. So why is it so hard for people to embrace storytelling in their own work?

I think there are two fundamental reasons. The first reason is that stories ask us to share emotion, which, to put it plainly, can be uncomfortable. If you're not used to it, it can feel like entering a foreign country where everyone speaks a different language and you have no map to find your way around. Or like walking into a social gathering where you don't know a single person. The whole experience can be daunting. But we also know how influential such experiences can be, how they can result in lifelong friendships and formative experiences.

The second fundamental reason people don't use stories is they don't know how. I know this may sound odd, because we are all storytellers. It's part of our genetic makeup. It's how our ancestors passed on knowledge. How we learned to hunt. How we learned to do *anything*. But somewhere along the way, the importance of storytelling and the skill of how to do it well have been lost. During the first industrial revolution, the education model changed. Schools were designed to focus on teaching skills to train engineers, lawyers, and doctors. If you weren't going into one of those three professions, you got a job in a trade. The importance of churning out workers overtook the need to share a story. This became the norm as those who went through school moved into the workplace. And the culture of school and work mirrored each other. So as we moved from an agrarian to industrial society, we lost the time and opportunity to connect through stories. Now, generations later, it's become a skill and tool only used by a select few.

So we don't use stories because emotion makes us feel uncomfortable and because we don't know how.

As for the first one, I say . . . get over it. Put yourself out there and learn from experience. It's only going to help you be a better communicator and a better leader. And for the second, in the next chapter, I am going to provide you with a tool that will help you successfully craft a story, every time.

We don't use
stories because

1 **emotion
makes us feel
uncomfortable**

2 **we don't
know how**

Remember

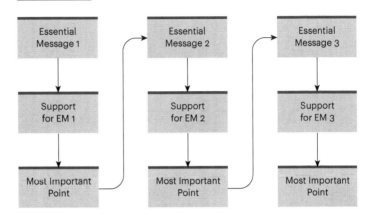

HOMEWORK

Before we dive into story, it's time to build out the rest of your Communication Canvas.

1 Write out your Essential Messages 1, 2, and 3. These should be short, in bullet-point form.

2 Next, write out your Support for Essential Messages 1, 2, and 3—facts, statistics, and stories. Again, keep them short.

3 Finally, write out your Most Important Point for each of your Essential Messages. This will seem repetitive!

This development order ensures you won't get stuck thinking about stories or examples that may or may not apply. Get the bulk of the structure down first.

6

THE STORY
SPINE

T HE MOVIE STUDIO Pixar has earned about $14 billion in revenues at the worldwide box office since it launched its very first movie, *Toy Story*, in 1995. Time and again the company, bought by Disney in 2006 for $7.4 billion, has delivered animated hit after hit after hit. From *Toy Story* to *Soul*, the Pixar team knows how to produce not just beautifully animated but perfectly crafted stories.

Although each one of these movies is different both visually and creatively, they all used the exact same model to develop the story: the Story Spine. The Story Spine is not a proprietary tool or technique created by Pixar; it was invented in 1991 by playwright Kenn Adams. Having seen short scenes improvised and turned into three-act productions, Adams had the idea to develop a technique to help artists write full-length plays. Since then, the Story Spine has been used by improvisers, creators, and storytellers to help them shape their work. There is a reason Pixar and so many others have embraced this method, and why you should too.

It works.

I want to take you back in time. Do you remember when, in the pre-COVIDian time when socializing was the norm, you were at a cocktail party, a dinner party, or a work function, and someone told a great story? Of course, you remember.

The story is well received, so someone else chimes in and shares their story, and it's good too. At this point, you may be sitting there thinking, "Oh! I have a story that really fits! I think it will go over well. I am going to share it!"

You pipe up and begin to tell your story. And as you are sharing, something terrible happens. The story is not coming out the way you want it to. Maybe you just can't remember a key part of the plot or perhaps you made a mistake and want to correct an earlier twist. Whatever the reason, by the time you get to the end, there is an awkward silence.

It lands with a silent thud on the floor. No one wants to look at the mess. You know it didn't go over well. You are slightly embarrassed. If you're lucky, the group will smile and thank you. But if you're unlucky, they will change the subject altogether. "Right. Did anyone watch the game last night?" You wonder, "What happened? What went wrong?"

You didn't use the Story Spine.

So what is the Story Spine? It's a structure to help you make sure you develop the strongest, most robust story possible. And it goes like this:

> Once upon a time there was a *character*
>
> And every day they *routine*
>
> Until one day *routine broken*
>
> Because of that *consequences*
>
> Because of that *consequences*
>
> Because of that *consequences*
>
> Until finally *success or failure*
>
> And ever since then *new routine*

The Story Spine gives you everything you need to be successful in your storytelling.

Once upon a time there was a **character**

↓

And every day they **routine**

↓

Until one day **routine broken**

↓

Because of that **consequences**

↓

Because of that **consequences**

↓

Because of that **consequences**

↓

Until finally **success or failure**

↓

And ever since then **new routine**

The beautiful thing about the Story Spine is it gives you everything you need to be successful in your storytelling:

Characters
Environment
Conflict
Raised conflict
Resolution

Let's use the story of *Toy Story* to see how this maps out.

Once upon a time there was a *toy named Sheriff Woody.*

And every day they *loved to play with their owner named Andy.*

Until one day *Andy got a new toy named Buzz Lightyear.*

Because of that *Andy played only with Buzz.*

Because of that *Woody got jealous and sad and left.*

Because of that *all the toys went to find Woody.*

Until finally *they convinced Woody that Andy would play with both of them.*

And ever since then *Andy has played with Woody and Buzz.*

This framework is not how you *recite* the story. Notice how it's fairly non-descriptive and lacks emotion? You will add that later. What the Story Spine does is create a solid framework to ensure your story has everything it needs. Here it is in the summary framework:

- Characters: Woody, Buzz, Andy, other toys
- Environment: House, Andy's room
- Conflict: New toy makes Woody jealous

- Raised conflict: Woody leaves
- Resolution: The other toys find Woody and discover they can all play together

The nice thing about the Story Spine is the details it creates. As my author friend Ian Donald Keeling likes to say, "It's not a tree. It's a giant oak." Using the Story Spine can get you to pull out the content *and* the details you need in order to create an emotional connection with your audience.

Use the Story Spine to help you develop your Lean In Moment. Find a story that is based on your experience or speaks to you personally *and* connects to your Purpose Statement.

COMMUNICATION CANVAS

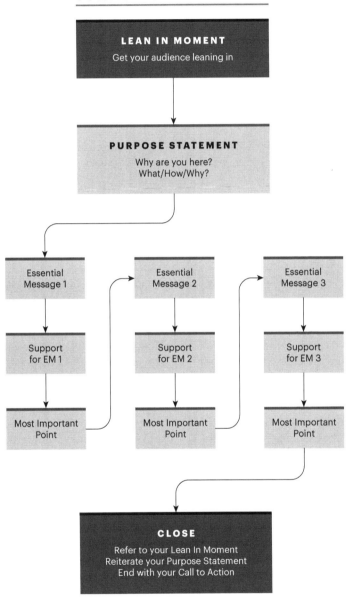

HOMEWORK

Your Communication Canvas is almost complete! Here's what you need to do next.

1 Download the Story Spine at impactbook.ca/tools.

2 Using the Story Spine, create your Lean In Moment.

3 Using the Story Spine, shape the stories in your Support for Essential Messages.

4 Write out your Close, which refers back to your Lean In Moment.

7

THE
POWER OF
EMOTIONAL
LANGUAGE

T HE STORY SPINE is a powerful tool, but what if you could create an emotional impact on your audience without having to tell an entire story? Fortunately, there are ways to engage the emotions of the audience that don't require an entire story. It's called rhetoric.

I first became aware of rhetoric when I was about eighteen years old and a camp counsellor at a summer camp in northern Ontario. It's the start of the day and I am with my seven campers at Camp Pine Crest in Torrance, Ontario, having ensured all the kids in my cabin have brushed their teeth after breakfast and are ready for the first activity. We are chatting and laughing, excited to be starting the day.

Then Aeschylus, a staff member and friend from high school, comes stomping by and he's upset. He has a newspaper in his hand; a news article has gotten him riled up. I ask him what's wrong and he replies, holding up the paper, "It's nothing but regurgitated rhetoric!" He stomps away before I could find out what had upset him. But I learned to love the sound of the phrase "regurgitated rhetoric."

But from that point on, I held a fairly negative view of the word. Rhetoric was language only used by politicians and those hoping to unfairly sway public opinion. I wasn't alone. To this day, when I ask attendees of my programs how they

Rhetoric helps translate complex ideas. And the world of work desperately needs translation.

feel about the word "rhetoric," many are unable to define it and most admit that they have a negative view of it.

Rhetoric is the use of emotional language to inform or persuade.

And I swear on my life, it's not such a bad thing! It's not a device only used by pushy salespeople and conniving politicians. While Aeschylus had every right to be upset about the news he'd read, rhetoric gets short shrift. Rhetoric is actually an instrument that can help translate complex ideas. And, as I argued earlier, the world of work desperately needs translation.

Below is a buffet of rhetorical devices that you can use in your presentations to make an emotional connection with your audience.

The Rhetorical Question

How are you sabotaging your presentations?

When I ask this question, especially in a presentation, I am not actually expecting a direct answer. It's a question that often prompts a series of thoughts and reflections. You might start by thinking, "What's he talking about? I don't sabotage anything!" But after a moment of reflection, "Well, maybe I could start preparing my presentations a little sooner." And after further thought, "I don't really rehearse."

The reality is, I don't want an answer. What I want is to kick-start your thought process and help you travel in your mind. Rhetorical questions are questions that don't require an answer but prompt an emotional or thoughtful reaction. They are questions we ask to create a dramatic effect or make a point.

My rhetorical question "How are you sabotaging your presentations?" may have shifted your thinking and perhaps made you feel insecure. Your mind may have started wandering. Where it went is inconsequential, but the journey started with the question. It tapped into the universal anxiety people have about preparing for presentations. The question created space for you to think and worry.

Often, presenters incorporate rhetorical questions off the top as a part of their Lean In Moment. This allows them to engage with the audience immediately and begin the journey their presentation will take them on. But we can also use rhetorical questions within the body of the presentation to illustrate the importance of an Essential Message. Or as a transitional tool to get to the next Essential Message, moving from one idea to another. For example, knowing that storytelling is a powerful tool, we might ask, "Are you willing to ignore this powerful technique?"

At the beginning of this chapter, I offered up a rhetorical question as a transitional device: "The Story Spine is a powerful tool, but what if you could create an emotional impact on your audience without having to tell an entire story?"

Rhetorical questions are very helpful but use them sparingly. When overused, they can become distracting and ineffective. Why would you want that?

Repetition

Repetition is an extremely effective rhetorical device.

Repetition is an extremely effective rhetorical device.

I used repetition earlier in this book to illustrate the importance of the Purpose Statement in the Communication Canvas. It may seem like an obvious tool to employ, yet the opportunity for repetition often presents itself and is ignored.

Repetition is an extremely effective rhetorical device. Repetition is an extremely effective rhetorical device. **Repetition is an** Repetition is an extremely effective rhetorical device. **extremely effective** Repetition is an extremely effective rhetorical device. **rhetorical device.** Repetition is an extremely effective rhetorical device. Repetition is an extremely effective rhetorical device.

It would be hard to find a better example of the use of rhetoric—in particular, repetition—than the famous "I Have a Dream" speech, which Dr. Martin Luther King Jr. delivered to more than 250,000 civil rights supporters from the steps of the Lincoln Memorial in Washington, D.C., on August 28, 1963. In it, Dr. King called for civil and economic rights and an end to racism in the United States. It was a defining moment of the civil rights movement and among the most iconic speeches in American history. It is also a masterpiece of rhetoric. If you haven't watched this speech in its entirety, I highly recommend you do.[1]

Dr. King says, "I still have a dream," then goes on to repeat the word "dream" eleven times in his speech. Dr. King could have simply explained the dream. Instead, he repeats "I have a dream" and describes the vision of the dream, back and forth from current reality to the potential future, taking the listener on a journey. It's a dream that we can participate in and travel into and along.

Beyond the emotional journey, the repetition of the phrase "I have a dream" drives home the important point in dramatic fashion. Again, like all rhetorical devices, use repetition judiciously so that when you do, it works.

My client Dr. Afsaneh Alavi, the dermatologist, successfully used repetition in her Lean In Moment: "Some of us dream of owning a bigger house. Some of us dream of winning the lottery. Some of us dream of world peace. And some of us dream ..." Like Dr. King, her opening included a contrast, not between the present and future, but between the dreams of healthy people and those suffering from HS.

Metaphors

Metaphors are implied comparisons between two unlike things and can create a sea of opportunity for you to connect with your audience.

See what I did there? Let's explore that metaphor, "a sea of opportunity." A "sea" and "opportunity" at first glance have nothing in common. One is the expanse of salt water that covers most of the Earth's surface while the other is a set of circumstances that makes it possible to do something. But upon closer inspection, the connections between "sea" and "opportunity" are many. A sea is vast, endless, and seemingly overwhelming. An opportunity can seem huge, endless, and overwhelming. Due to the sea's ever-changing state, it can be bumpy, choppy, hard to navigate, and daunting. An opportunity can feel hard to navigate and daunting. The sea can be stunningly beautiful and breathtaking. So can an opportunity.

Metaphors can be so powerful that some companies fully embrace them and incorporate them into their branding or messaging. "Red Bull Gives You Wings" is one great example. Budweiser's "The King of Beers" is another.

Similes

Similes are an implied comparison between two unlike things using "like" or "as." Similes are like the unexpected guest at a dinner party. They provide zest, life, a unique perspective, and seem to appear out of nowhere. Many similes are ubiquitous in conversation. Here are a few common examples:

- You were as brave as a lion.
- They fought like cats and dogs.
- Your explanation is as clear as mud.

Like metaphors, similes have been embraced by businesses. General Motors' campaign tagline for their Chevy trucks, "Like a Rock," is a great example. But original similes can help people understand something that is truly different. My brother is a screenwriter and producer in Hollywood. His job is not just to write and produce new series but to pitch them. To explain a new series, he often brings together two well-known shows to illustrate the concept.

Ozark is like *Breaking Bad* meets *Justified*.

Rick and Morty is like *Family Guy* meets *Futurama* meets *Robot Chicken*.

This tool is not just for ad agencies and Hollywood screenwriters, it can be used to describe anything:

An iPhone is like a computer married your phone.

Social media is like the company water cooler: people come to get the latest news.

Our AI software is like the filing cabinet for your law firm.

Out of all the rhetorical devices, metaphors and similes are the ones that can most easily and effortlessly translate the complex into simple, understandable concepts. They are there at your disposal, so dive in and use them.

I know I sound like a broken record, but use them sparingly.

Diacope

Want to drive a point home and create a bit of an unconscious emotional stir with your audience? Try using a diacope. What is a diacope?

A repetition. A repetition. A repetition with an interruption. A repetition. That's what diacope is.

Dr. King uses diacope to perfection to close out his "I Have a Dream" speech. He says, "Free at last. Free at last. Thank God almighty, we are free at last."

Diacope is a great tool to drive home a point with a sense of emotional urgency.

Humour

And what about humour? What about making people laugh so they feel more comfortable? For many, it's easier said than done. I can tell you one thing: trying to write about humour is probably one of the unfunniest things you can do. That being said, I want to share my two cents on humour, why I believe it's important to use, and how anyone can incorporate it into a presentation, talk, or pitch.

Earlier in my career, I was part of Urban Myth, a comedy troupe based out of Toronto. We performed regularly at the legendary Rivoli and Second City and toured and performed on stages across the country. For a brief time, we even had a TV show called *SketchCom*. We all worked collaboratively as writers, actors, and directors bringing absurd, sometimes darkly comedic sketches to life on stage. Our inspirations were Kids in the Hall, Monty Python, and *Saturday Night Live*.

We had some terrifically funny sketches, like "The Amputated Hand" about a family that runs a sawmill, each member missing a variety of limbs, on their way to the hospital. Another sketch, "Blind Date," shared a series of vignettes about a man whose date got sick, so he's out with her surrogate, her gung-ho older brother. Armed with a box of conversation starter cue cards, they make their way from pick-up to dinner and eventually the bedroom, only by using the cue cards. In execution, both sketches were very funny and always well received. The fundamental reason: they accessed the truth.

I share these examples not because I want you to develop sketches or jokes, but to drive home the point that truth matters. Unless you are a gifted joke teller, I wouldn't bother writing or telling jokes. Instead, take the time to find the shared human experience with your audience. Nervous? Let them confidently know. Excited? Tell them! Likely, your audience will be able to relate.

Just to clarify, you are not looking for people to laugh. It would be great if they did, as laughing helps to relax the audience and you as well. All you are looking for, all that is needed, is a smile. From some of them. Like laughter, smiling gets them on your side. They are with you. They support you. And they are encouraging you.

So unless Jerry Seinfeld is your father, don't try to create and tell jokes. Share common experiences. Share universal perspectives. And if you find something funny, don't just share it, show it. Laughing at your story will encourage the audience to laugh too.

A few years ago, I delivered a talk to a group of tech leaders in Toronto on how to communicate with impact. I was encouraging the group of two hundred engineers and technologists to communicate with emotion, using emotional language. After I finished, I had a lineup of people who wanted to connect, ask questions, and exchange contact information. At the end of the line was Dennis. His name tag was on upside down and he, unlike all the others, wasn't smiling. I tilted my head to read his name and asked Dennis where he was from.

He didn't answer but told me he thought I was full of shit. I was taken aback. I have people ask me challenging questions all the time, but Dennis came on strong. I said, "I am sorry you feel that way. Can you explain why you think I am full of shit?"

He replied that using emotional language was something that could *never* happen in his work. He had been running a number of businesses for over ten years, and if he ever used emotional language, his clients would revolt.

I smiled. And I thanked him for his feedback. And then I pointed out that he had been using emotional language since we started chatting. I pointed out that "full of shit" was a metaphor, as was the fact that his clients would "revolt." Dennis smiled, said he still disagreed, and then wandered into the crowd.

The fact is emotional language is inescapable. It creeps into our conversation. Into our business language. Into our minds. And we shouldn't be afraid to use these tools. Remember, your sensory cortex activates when you hear metaphors or other rhetorical devices. Rhetoric is a tool, along with storytelling, that can help us tap into the hearts and minds of our audience. And it's free.

The tools at your fingertips to simplify and transform your pitch and presentation include the Communication Canvas, the Purpose Practice, the Story Spine, and emotional language or rhetoric. Now it's the time to put them all together to finish your talk.

COMMUNICATION CANVAS

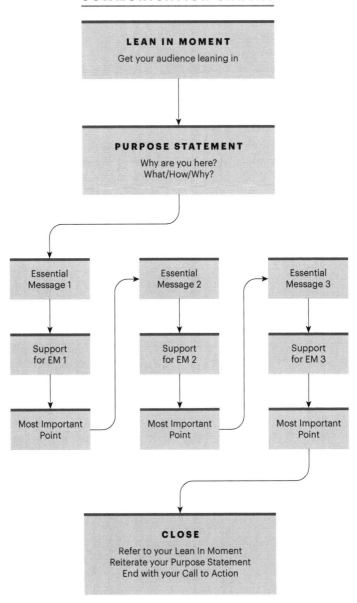

LEAN IN MOMENT
Get your audience leaning in

PURPOSE STATEMENT
Why are you here?
What/How/Why?

Essential Message 1

Essential Message 2

Essential Message 3

Support for EM 1

Support for EM 2

Support for EM 3

Most Important Point

Most Important Point

Most Important Point

CLOSE
Refer to your Lean In Moment
Reiterate your Purpose Statement
End with your Call to Action

HOMEWORK

1   Review the rough draft of your Communication Canvas and
    flesh out your bullet-point notes into a full draft.

2   As you are doing so, identify spots where you can integrate
    rhetorical devices by asking:

●   Do I want to take the audience on a journey? Could I ask a
    rhetorical question?
●   Will a metaphor help communicate this?
●   Is there an opportunity to instill emotion?

3   Finish revising your talk! Use your accountability partner if
    you need to!

8

TELL YOUR STORY

AM NERVOUS. It's 2014 and I'm sitting in the office of one of the world's greatest regenerative scientists, Dr. Molly Shoichet. Dr. Shoichet holds the Canada Research Chair in tissue engineering at the University of Toronto. She has published more than five hundred papers and given hundreds and hundreds of lectures worldwide. She leads a laboratory that has graduated more than two hundred scientists. In addition, Molly is actively engaged in translational research and science outreach and in 2015 won a L'Oréal–UNESCO For Women in Science International Award. She holds the Order of Ontario and is the former chief scientist of Ontario. Molly, as they say, is no slouch.

And I am sitting in her office, outside the lab where she and her team are trying to find cures for stroke and blindness. What is this film/theatre graduate doing with one of the world's most recognized and celebrated regenerative medicine scientists? I have been asked to coach Molly on the talk she's delivering at TEDxToronto in a few short months.

It turns out Molly is nervous too. Not about her work. The work that was coming out of her lab was truly remarkable. Among other things, her team had developed a potentially game-changing polymer that could help to heal the blood-brain barrier after a stroke. The question facing us isn't "Does Molly have something to talk about?" The question is "Which breakthrough should Molly talk about and how on earth could she explain it so the lay audience understands?"

We dive in. And, slowly but surely, we land on her Purpose Statement. Then we build out the rest of the Communication Canvas framework. After about a month of solid coaching sessions and Molly focusing on writing and developing her talk, she has a strong rough framework. It's time to develop the Lean In Moment and integrate story and rhetoric throughout.

Her talk is about how she uses engineering methodology to solve medical problems and take a personalized approach to medical solutions: "We have the opportunity to design strategies for the individual, going beyond treating the symptoms of disease and even reversing it. This is the promise of personalized medicine."

After much discussion with me probing and asking about her history, childhood, and other experiences, she lands on a personal story. She shares that as a child she performed in a play, written by her brother. Her line at the end of the play was to ask all the adults in the world, "Isn't it time for a change?" This is it: the story she should share at the beginning of her talk, adding, "This question has stayed with me and shaped my work and my career."

In her talk, she covers some pretty complex topics: the challenge of growing cancer cells to treat patients, overcoming blindness, and the need to heal the brain after it's damaged by stroke. Each of her Essential Messages unpacks these areas and the personalized treatment that is possible, using metaphor and simile.

She explains that hyaluronic acid is found in many cancer tissues and is a good material to grow cancer cells in the lab. Hyaluronic acid is "a little bit like molasses." Hello, simile! She then shares, "Unlike Jell-O, simply cooling it in the refrigerator would not work." Molly finishes her talk by revisiting her opening story, closing with "In the future, we will wonder why it took us so long to make a change."

It is engaging and satisfying **to watch a story unfold throughout a talk.**

Can you integrate a unifying story so it is woven throughout your talk? The short answer is: of course! It's a challenging task that requires more time and effort. But it can be very engaging and satisfying to watch a story unfold throughout a talk, especially if the story helps reinforce a key message or shares supporting messages. Molly did a terrific job of using all the tools in the toolbelt.

Here's the dirty truth about delivering presentations: shit happens. Just like in life, anything can happen. The fire alarm can go off. The power can go off. Someone's phone can too. Or the audience could have just been given bad news. But when it all comes together and you rehearse, it can feel incredible. It also means you can pretty much face anything. I love this story a client shared with me. It is a wonderful example of presentation success: My client arrived at the venue to discover that he was presenting at the very end of a full-day program— and just before the open bar reception! Shaken, he took to the stage, but the moment he got up there, the notes on the comfort monitor vanished and he had to rely on doing everything from memory. Yet because he had rehearsed and rehearsed and rehearsed, he said his stories flowed from opening to purpose to close. He received accolades from the audience, and he felt like it was the best presentation he had ever delivered. He felt great and, more importantly, it had rekindled his passion for public speaking!

This is not just a story of presentation success. It's a story of leadership. The Simplify and Transform principles of the Path to Impact work in tandem to help you can handle anything that comes your way because you know your stuff! In the final part of this book—Perform—we explore how to perform no matter where you are or who you are presenting to.

HOMEWORK

Read through the first draft of your talk and ask yourself:

- Is it clear and simple?

- Is my Purpose Statement as clear as it can be? Is it strong?

- Do all my Essential Messages support it?

- Are there stories or a story integrated throughout?

- Am I proud of the presentation?

- Is it right?

If you feel you can make it better, then go for it! Take another pass at revising your draft.

PART 3

PERFORM
PERFORM
PERFORM

PERFORM

PERFORM
PERFORM
PERFORM

9

BEHIND THE CURTAIN

ALL THE WORLD'S A STAGE. I believe some guy named Shakespeare once said that. The reality is, once you have a script, only then can you start to focus on *how* you are going to deliver that script. Now that you've completed the Simplify and Transform parts of the Path to Impact, you're ready to focus on the production.

Shakespeare also wrote, "To thine own self be true." If we are being honest, performance seems to be one area where many people ignore that advice. They often think that preparation is unnecessary, that they can "wing it." That expression, "to wing it," comes from the theatre, alluding to an actor studying their part in the wings (the areas to either side of the stage) because they have been suddenly called on to replace another actor. Is that how you want to show up? No! You want to come across professionally, confident, like there is no other place you would rather or should be!

I believe that performance is essential, whether you're on a phone call, in a coffee meeting, or delivering a keynote presentation. Your presentation must be grounded in performance.

When I was first starting my career, I found myself in a job where I didn't fit. I was a recent alum of an undergraduate arts program in theatre and film from Queen's University, which I followed up with a bachelor of education. I was also a

DO NOT DO NOT

DO NOT DO NOT

DO NOT DO NOT

DO NOT DO NOT

DO NOT DO NOT

DO NOT DO NOT

DO NOT DO NOT

DO NOT DO NOT

just wing it.

big fan of environmental education, having spent quite a bit of my youth camping and working in outdoor recreation.

It was because of my education and my environmental background that an engineering firm asked me to join their team to help them deliver a unique environmental education program. After a few months, they asked if I would sell and promote the program as well. Little did I know this was something that I was ill prepared for.

It wasn't that I didn't believe in the program or wasn't well versed in the content—the problem was I loved film and theatre and working in an engineering firm made me feel very much out of place in the world. And I developed a strange, physical tic.

It first appeared when I was presenting to the vice president of the company, Gary, and the president of the company, Tom. I was sharing what we hoped to accomplish with the program and our plan. My colleague, Helen, looked at me wide-eyed, as if I'd said something really, really weird. After the presentation, as we were leaving the boardroom, I turned to her and asked, "Did I say something wrong? Why did you look at me like that?"

She said, "No, it wasn't that. What were you doing with your mouth? You literally had your mouth stretching out . . . almost like a beak." I didn't know what she was talking about.

A week later I was delivering another presentation, and Helen smiled at me and indicated that it was happening again. I realized that I had a tic. When something unconsciously didn't feel right, my beak would emerge: my lips would push out for about a half second and then pull back.

Many of us have our own "beak." It can come in the form of an always-shaking leg. Or wandering the stage or boardroom. There's the blinker. Or some people have verbal tics that they repeat like "um" or "er." I call those filler words.

I'm lucky that I had Helen, giving me the heads-up that my beak was showing. Turns out that friend was a very good friend, indeed. I ended up marrying Helen. And we've been together for almost twenty-five years!

I was generating a beak because I felt like I didn't fit in, that I was a fraud. From that point on, I started to think about my presentations in a different way. I started to think about them as performances. Every single one of them was important. Every single one required preparation.

You need to start thinking about yourself as a performer. No matter who you are or where you are. Whether you're at home on Zoom or Teams, on a stage, or in a boardroom for a job interview, you are performing. Those places are your communication spaces. I want you to start thinking about how to set yourself up for success every single time you present or communicate.

We need to know where we will be performing to set ourselves up for success. Whenever I am delivering a talk or a pitch or a workshop, I do a site inspection. I want to ensure that the space is what was described in the booking call or, if booked through an agent, in my rider. I like to be able to plug in my own computer, use a clicker, and ensure all audio and video are working.

Here's why. It's not always exactly what we agreed to. The laptop isn't available. They have the wrong file. There is no table. Or no podium. Whatever the challenge may be, I need to be able to pivot and still deliver a great presentation.

Historically, you would be going to a boardroom or a stage to deliver a presentation. In today's environment, with COVID, there is a good chance you will need to deliver your presentation via videoconferencing from your home office, living room, or dining room table. In this case, the audio-visual setup will not be someone else's responsibility. It will be yours! You must still create a *performance* space where you look and sound your best. There are a number of things you can do to make that happen.

Elevate Your Camera

Most computers have a camera at the top of the screen, which positions the camera lower than your face, likely at chest level. That means the camera is tilting up and you are likely looking down into the camera. The audience or your team is getting a great shot of your throat and chin and, if they are really unlucky, up your nostrils!

Unless you are aiming for an artsy or dramatic effect, which you are not, your camera should be aimed at your face, positioned higher than your eyes, at approximately the same level as your forehead.

There are lots of terrific computer stands to be found out there. But if you don't want to spend the money buying a stand, no problem. Go to your bookshelf and get a half-dozen hardcover books, and place your computer on top. Do this carefully! Or use a box. That should do it. Raised computer. Raised camera. A better-looking you!

Lighting the Space

Have you ever taken a photo that you just love? It's captured a moment, people, a place, an experience that was just perfect. A number of years ago, I was delivering a program in New York City. One evening, I exited the subway in the Village (near my favourite comedy club on the planet) and began walking back to my hotel. I was tired but happy. I stopped on the corner of

6th Avenue and Minetta and looked down the street. What I saw seemed, to me anyway, just beautiful. I reached for my phone and took a picture.

At first glance, it's nothing special. It's a deserted New York City street. There's a Mexican restaurant. A fallen bicycle. A few trees. But when I saw what I had captured, I loved it. I shared it with my family; they loved it. My friends loved it. It's been blown up and now hangs in my dining room. What makes this photo great? The lighting! Darkness pervades the image. A spot of yellow light in the middle lights up space. Splashes of light from the sides. The road shimmers. The lighting makes something mundane beautiful. Think I am full of malarkey? A year later I found myself on the same corner in the early afternoon. So I snapped another picture.

It's fine, but it's kind of plain and the magic is completely missing. Lighting matters! When I am delivering an online keynote or workshop, I have a setup designed to help me look and sound my best. I have multiple lights, microphones, and, depending on the event, a couple of different cameras. But not everyone has the luxury of investing in gear, nor do you need to! Lighting in your space is very important as it will give even a lower-grade camera or poor internet connection a better, more professional look. It's pretty simple. Make sure there is enough light above or around you, and most importantly, ensure you have a light *behind* your computer.

A no-no: the window seat! While a window may be a nice place to work as it provides you with natural light and you can see the world around you, it's one of the *worst* places to present. Avoid sitting in front of a window or anywhere with lights behind you. You'll look like you're part of a witness protection program, a silhouette that your meeting participants won't be able to see clearly.

What's Your Background?

If you can't have that awesome window behind you, what can you do? Anything is better than nothing. A bookshelf works. A plant or two. Something decorative. If you can avoid it, don't use a plain background, unless it's well lit.

Finally, when you're presenting from home, ensure you've got some privacy. A closed door to block out the traffic of partners, kids, or pets and to reduce the sound from other parts of your home.

Decide what your "presentation look" is going to be, know how you can capture it, and then move on. You've got to prepare!

It's All about Your Image (and How You Sound)

One of the things I like to do in preparation for any talk is arrive early and take a walk on the stage. I check my entrance and exit points and sightlines, as well as test my tech.

Whether you're in front of a live audience on stage or on screen, the fundamental questions you need to ask yourself are:

Can Everyone See Me and Hear Me?

Does the mic work? Like good lighting, having a good camera and microphone *does* make a difference. There are lots of excellent webcams on the market and many tablets and laptops come with excellent cameras and microphones built in. Ensure your camera is working. Ensure your microphone is working.

Can Everyone See Me Clearly?

Are there any blind spots? The person who can't see you could be an important decision maker! Walking the stage allows you to see if there are any blind spots for yourself or the audience. Determine where you will be entering and exiting from. A walkabout also allows you to envision yourself delivering your talk.

If you're delivering virtually, is anyone having trouble seeing you? How do you appear when you pop on screen and how does the audience appear? Are people using their cameras? If not, encourage them to turn them on.

Do My Visuals Work?

Can I clearly and easily share my presentation and any video? When you're delivering remotely, jump on the software in advance, whether it's Zoom, Microsoft Teams, Skype, or GoToMeeting, and *test it out*. Are you comfortable navigating the software, moving your presentation forward or backward, sharing your screen, and engaging your audience using polls, chat, or Q&A functions?

Camera? Check.
Sound? Check.
Lighting? Check.
Presentation? Check.

Take it upon yourself to carve out the time to ensure these questions are answered. Run a test presentation or technical rehearsal with your client, a colleague, or do it on your own.

Being prepared means showing up *early*. Asking these questions does not make you a prima donna. It simply shows you care about providing the best value and giving the best presentation to your audience.

Living Your Story

Many years ago, when I was running a mid-sized communication and events company out of Toronto, I found myself

Camera?

Sound?

Lighting?

Presentation? ✓

shooting a video with a dozen or so leaders from AstraZeneca, one of the world's largest pharmaceutical companies. At their upcoming national sales meeting, we were going to share stories from leaders from across the country. Each story was going to be unique, almost like a commercial, and touch upon a key value that the company embraced.

I was very proud of all the stories we produced. They were incredible. But one in particular stands out. Maureen was a senior sales leader who had a story to tell about her struggle with cancer. It was a sensitive subject as she was only one year clear of it. She was healthy, but speaking about it brought back the hardship she had lived through. We had the entire video crew and production set up. A number of lights. A couple of cameras. A chair for her to sit comfortably. And a largish team, including cameraperson, lighting designer, sound technician, makeup person, and a producer/interviewer.

Maureen was getting settled, and the makeup person was applying finishing touches. The videographer started to set up the shots, and the producer, Nathalie, chatted with Maureen to get her comfortable, asking her about her story. Maureen shared a little at first about her work, but then she moved into how she had struggled with cancer. It was terrifying. But her colleagues were with her every step of the way, even driving her to chemo and bringing her home. Maureen finished telling her story. We were all silent. It was touching. It was beautiful. It held meaning for us and we didn't even know Maureen or work for the company.

She took a breath and asked, "Should we get started?" But we were already done. We had filmed the entire story in rehearsal, while she was getting her makeup on. It was one of the best story videos I have ever produced.

Maureen knew her story. She had lived it. She had shared it before. And we had created a stage for her to tell it. We need to be like Maureen when we are presenting. We need to be comfortable with our content and relaxed with the people and the technology, so we can confidently share our content, regardless of what is going on around us.

If someone isn't going to do it for you, create your own stage. Think about the sound, visuals, sightlines, the look and feel you want to deliver. Use all the tools at your disposal to bring your presentation to life and set yourself up for success.

HOMEWORK

Download the Getting Speaker Ready Checklist from
impactbook.ca/tools, and then run through a technical
rehearsal as if you are about to present.

- Make sure your camera is elevated slightly higher than
  eye level.

- Ensure the light is behind your camera/computer.

- Make sure there are no windows behind you.

- Frame your head and shoulders on screen. Is your
  camera working?

- Is your microphone is working?

- Are your headphones working?

- Are your visuals ready?

- Are you clear of noise or distractions (if possible)?

- Are you grateful for the opportunity to present?

10

THE USE
OF VISUALS

AM SITTING WITH a well-respected CEO. He's a brilliant tactician and strategist. He's well read in all areas of the agile software development process. He's got an encyclopedic ability to recite details, facts, and knowledge from any book or textbook he's ever read. We've spent a few weeks developing a Communication Canvas for his upcoming forty-minute keynote at a large McKinsey conference. We are diving into the rehearsal portion and he's worried about his slides. I can see he wants to talk about this. He has put some thought into it. So we dive in.

He opens up the deck that he spent the weekend preparing. It's over 150 slides. It has every kind of graph known to man. It has slides with lines and lines and lines of text.

He has methodically picked out slides from his past presentations, a few from this and a few from that, modifying some of them. For every single point of his supporting messaging, he has a slide or two. Sometimes three.

To embrace a metaphor: it was a dog's breakfast.

I smiled and I asked him the *five questions*. These five questions will ensure you have what you need and only what you need on your slides. And here they are, the five questions you need to ask yourself about each and every slide:

1 Is it additive?
2 Will it simplify?
3 Will it transform?
4 Does it look good?
5 Will the visual help me perform?

These five questions, if answered honestly, will keep your presentation from losing its shape. Let's go through them, one by one.

1. Is It Additive?

I get asked time and again, "What do I put on my slides?" My answer is the same. Every time. Nothing. Use no visuals. At all. Nada. Not a sausage.

Am I being a facetious? Yes, but only a tad. The reality is most of the time you don't need visuals. A great TED Talk doesn't incorporate visuals. It uses stories. A great speaker can hold the attention of the audience without visuals. Your visuals are often referred to as "speaker support" for a reason.

Ask yourself, "What extra value does this slide provide to the audience?" Is it providing a behind-the-scenes sneak peek at something the audience would normally never get to see? Is it a wonderful gem of insight that drives your key message home?

If so, then put it in. But, more often than not, our visuals are just duplication or filler. Challenge yourself to use less and share more from the stage.

2. Will It Simplify?

Sometimes a good visual helps to create clarity. Listing off numbers in a financial model can be a dry experience for the audience and difficult to follow. Showing some numbers can help to simplify and create understanding. Far too often, people love sharing their data slides (which are important!) but they show *all* the data. The definition of "simplify" is to make something simpler or easier to do or understand. When showing data in an effort to simplify, ensure you aren't unintentionally doing the opposite.

Share data only if it's additive. Remove complexities from it. Zoom in on or visually highlight the specific data or areas of focus and share only that. This way you add to your point and simplify simultaneously.

3. Will It Transform?

Sometimes a slide creates a deeper level of connection or engagement with the audience. Transforming the content is all about using story or, in this case, a visual story to engage your audience in a different way. Does this visual have the ability to connect and transform the audience or the content to create context?

Oren Berkovich, CEO of SingularityU Canada, delivers wonderful presentations and programs on the importance of mindset when embracing change. His slides are always immaculate and beautifully designed. He shares that you can have a planning mindset or an experimentation mindset, for example. There are polarities in mindset, and you can be leading or learning. You can embrace a mindset of scarcity or one of abundance. During one presentation, Oren focused on how it is possible to have two mindsets simultaneously.

You may be scratching your head. How is it possible to have two mindsets? To illustrate his point, he shared an image of an optical illusion. You may have seen it before. It was a drawing of an old woman with a head scarf on. But if you stared at it in a different way, you could see it was a drawing of a young woman, just slightly turned away.

He waited until people could see both and then said, "Now you see both the old woman and the young woman, you can move back and forth between them. It's something you've trained yourself to do very quickly. We can do the same with mindsets."

A very powerful point. And a well-placed and well-timed visual connected and created context for his audience. Using visual storytelling, Oren was able to skillfully transform the presentation for the audience.

4. Does It Look Good?

Yes, it needs to look good. You are asking people to look at the slide. If you were to go out to dinner, whether it was a Michelin three-star restaurant or a diner, and they dropped a plate in front of you that looked terrible, you would raise your eyebrows, ask a question or two, or send it back.

The same is true with our slides. If it looks bad, people will tune out. If it is hard to follow, people will want to interrupt to ask questions. And not the good kind. If your slides are bad, the audience can't treat you like a dish at a restaurant and send you back. But they can, like a customer at a restaurant, leave, either mentally or physically.

Ask yourself, "Does this look good? Do I like it? Can I make it look better? Would I put the image on my wall or keep it on my desk as memorabilia?"

If so, great! Keep it. If not, improve it!

5. Will the Visual Help Me Perform?

When I am teaching my Communication Canvas, I often show the framework in its entirety. I show this visual so people understand that it's a framework as well as a process. It is a vital tool that helps leaders communicate, and without the visual, my presentation becomes hard to follow. So I share the whole thing. I show the Communication Canvas in its entirety, and then I zoom in on the Purpose Practice on a separate slide as I break down the process step by step. I treat it like a map highlighting the journey we are taking together as well as our final destination.

A visual can help you perform. It can be a photo that illustrates a moment. Or a comedic experience. Or a setting. But one should do it. You don't need to show photo after photo through your story. One should suffice—if it doesn't, change the story.

Remember the five questions:

1 Is it additive?
2 Will it simplify?
3 Will it transform?
4 Does it look good?
5 Do I need this visual to help me perform?

They will ensure your audience is focused on you and not the screen.

The five questions you need to ask yourself about each and every slide:

1 **Is it additive?**

2 **Will it simplify?**

3 **Will it transform?**

4 **Does it look good?**

5 **Will the visual help me perform?**

HOMEWORK

Begin developing your visuals.

1 Choose your software: PowerPoint, Keynote, or other.

2 For every section of your Communication Canvas, ask yourself the five questions of your slides.

3 When you are done, do a practice run of your presentation
   by reading your talk and clicking through the slides. Does
   anything not fit? Is there anything missing?

11

CLAIMING YOUR SPACE

MANY OF YOU will know Kelsey Grammer from his time playing Dr. Frasier Crane on the classic 1980s sitcom *Cheers* and then on his own successful sitcom *Frasier*, which still hold up today as examples of great comedy writing. Before Kelsey Grammer made it big on *Cheers* and *Frasier*, he was a stage actor. I had the privilege of seeing him interviewed live on stage at the Banff World Television Festival a number of years ago and heard him share this story.

Kelsey was performing in *Othello* at the Stratford Festival, sharing the stage with esteemed Canadian actor Christopher Plummer. Kelsey was young and nervous, perhaps even a bit timid. Plummer was a force to be reckoned with and wouldn't let anyone get in his way, especially a young timid actor. During each performance, Plummer would take his place and if Kelsey was unsure of his spot on stage, Plummer would literally push him where he wanted him to be. One time, Plummer pushed Kelsey so hard he broke his foot.

A few weeks later, during a matinee performance, Kelsey was once again being manhandled by Mr. Plummer and suddenly had had enough. He lost it and got so angry he actually threw Plummer off the stage.

Plummer came storming back on stage and Kelsey thought, "Well, that's it. I'm fired." Far from it. From that point on, they had an incredible time. They became friends. The performance improved. Kelsey had claimed his space.

To claim your space, you don't need to throw anyone or anything off the stage. You simply need to use your body to show your audience that you are comfortable and you belong.

Status

I am begging for change. I need money to get home. I walk up to a passerby and try to get his attention. He ignores me so I follow him and ask if he has any change. He smiles at the other people around him but completely ignores me. I try again and again to get his attention. "Sir, I really need to get home, do you have any change?" But he will have nothing to do with me. He won't help me. I feel small. I try again. "My wife and child are depending on me. I spent my last dollars on these diapers and they need me to get home. Do you have any—" Quickly and without warning, the man turns to me and, looking down at me, says, "I don't have any time, money, or resources for someone like . . . you." He says the last part with a sneer on his face. As he glares down at me, I shrink lower to the ground.

The man is James Roussel and, thankfully, he is a friend. We are in our third week of the Level 1 Improvisation class at Second City in Toronto. Our instructor, Jenny Parsons, had the class engage in an exercise focusing on status. Little did I know that over the next few years James and our classmates Todd Aiken and Aurora Browne would be taking these skills to countless stages across the country and on television with our comedy troupe Urban Myth. And the concept of status would stay with me.

Years later, while working with a group of pharmaceutical executives on their presentation skills, I decided to integrate status into my program as the entryway to body language.

The word "status" conjures up all kinds of figures, concepts, and emotions, from royalty and top-level execs to inequality and helplessness. When exploring status, people might connect the concept with images of the Queen or Bill Gates, or heart-breaking commercials with starving children or the homeless. Although I won't be delving into the inequality gap in this book, it is precisely because of these feelings and associated images that it is important to consider the implications of status.

Status can be defined as the relative social, professional, or other standing of someone or something, and it's the "other standing" part I want to touch upon. Status is the way you hold yourself at work, at home, or in your community: the physical manifestation of your status.

How you stand, how you position your body on screen, on stage, or in the boardroom affects how people perceive you.

Think of status like a scale, one being the lowest and ten being the highest. The lower the status, the more pronounced the physical manifestation. The same is true with the elements of higher status.

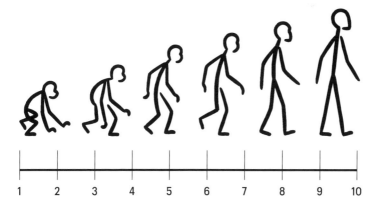

The physical indicators of low status can be seen in:

- Sloped shoulders
- Hunched back
- Chin down
- No eye contact
- Lower to the ground
- Asymmetric arms and legs

The physical indicators of high status are literally the opposite:

- Shoulders back
- Erect back and spine
- Chin straight or up
- Direct eye contact
- Standing straight and tall
- Symmetry in your arms and legs

We are often unaware of the fact that our body is communicating a certain status level because we unconsciously react to our environment, which consists of a myriad of inputs. So much happens from the time you wake up to the time you make it to your first meeting. And it can all affect your mental and physical state. There's the weather, the news (personal or professional), and interactions with family, friends, or strangers. Even a look from someone can cause some people's status to change.

Imagine you are leaving your house to deliver a presentation. You've planned it, your content is rock solid, you've rehearsed it, and you're ready to go. Unfortunately, on the way, you get into a fender bender. Or you get out of the taxi and get splashed with slush. Or you walk into the office and get a ping on your phone and learn that the deal you were hoping for didn't close.

Use your body to show
your audience that

↓

**you are
comfortable**

↓

and you belong.

All these things impact your status. They affect your mind and your body. So it behooves us to think about how we are holding ourselves before we go on stage or on screen. What is your "other standing"?

Ask yourself, "Is this how I want to be seen? Is this how I want to show up?"

Lowering Your Status

I am nervously placing our flip chart and markers around the room. Dale is standing in front of a room of custodial staff. We have delivered about twenty different workshops already to different clients. We always wear jackets and ties. We always stand when we present, and we always make it fun. But today is different. There is tension in the room. The audience is not happy.

Remember my first job? The one where I developed a beak? My role was to engage key stakeholders, principals, teachers, custodians, and students, to embrace something new: the three Rs—Reduce, Reuse, and Recycle. (This story reveals my age!) I designed and delivered programs that encouraged each stakeholder to raise awareness and become environmental stewards by setting up recycling, composting, and reduction campaigns. This may sound basic, but it was fairly new back then, during a time when school board budgets were being cut dramatically. The end result was a reduction in costs while doing something that helped our planet.

That morning Dale and I had been travelling up north from Toronto to the Simcoe County Board of Education to deliver a workshop to one group of stakeholders, the custodial staff. The custodians are essential to the success of the program and, at our request, the superintendent of operations had assembled approximately a hundred of them from across the region.

Dale is more senior than me and experienced in the field of building environments. He is a technologist; I am an educator. Both of us have strong creative sides and we get along and work well together. We like putting ourselves out there to connect with students, teachers, principals, and custodial staff. We make learning fun.

We were about twenty minutes away from the board office when Dale received a phone call. It is one of those moments when you just know something is wrong. Dale said, "Oh. Oh. Oh no. That's a real shame. So sorry to hear that. Okay. We will. Thanks." He hung up.

"What happened?" I asked. "Everything okay?"

"Approximately 50 percent of the custodial staff across the school board were laid off yesterday."

The information hung in the air as we let the news sink in. It felt heavy around us.

We have a workshop planned with exercises, tools, and props. (Yes, props. We make learning fun, remember?) But this is *not* be the time or place to deliver the program we had designed. Yet the request from the board is to deliver the program as planned.

Before I knew it, we arrived at our destination. As I unloaded the van, I asked Dale, "What's our plan? I mean, we can't just deliver our regular program, can we?"

He said, like something out of a cool cop show, "Just follow my lead." And I do.

Entering the room, we see forty-five custodians huddled in smaller groups having coffee. There are chairs spread out, but no one is seated. We set everything up—projector, markers, flip chart, handouts. Then it is time to present. I follow Dale's lead.

Is this how I
want to be seen?
**Is this how I want
to show up?**

Dale takes off his jacket and removes his tie. He rolls up his sleeves. He brings a chair to the front of the room, turns it around, and sits in it in reverse so he is facing the group with his arms resting on the chair back casually. He looks down. Then he raises his head up to the group and says, "We are here today representing the board, and our workshop is going to cover some of the actions we want you to take in your schools in order to help our planet and the school board reduce costs."

There is a murmuring.

"But we know today and the rest of the week will be very hard. We were informed of the changes made in the board yesterday, so we are going to do things a little differently. We do need to share some information with you, but we will do this quickly in about ten to fifteen minutes. Then we will answer any questions you may have. Any questions you may have that we can't answer, we'll take them back to the superintendent. We want to ensure your questions are heard and answered."

Not only did Dale signal his deference by removing the typical uniform of status, but he also literally got lower to the ground. He lowered his chin and dropped his eyes to the ground to begin, then raised them to make eye contact, back hunched and arms asymmetrical by resting them on the back of the chair.

Within minutes he has the group talking and sharing. They are upset, some of them have their voices raised, but most express their concerns and appreciate the opportunity to be heard. We capture every word and put it in our report so the superintendent is aware of the ideas and suggestions from the team. It was masterful.

Setting Your Status

Dale was able to shift his status to meet the needs of our audience. It doesn't matter that this group was custodial staff—they could have been pilots or sales reps or any group that has just had their peers let go due to restructuring.

An external attack on status can come at any time, from anywhere, so how can you ensure your standing is where you want it to be, and how do you prepare yourself?

The first thing to ask yourself is, "How do I want to show up?" Do you want to show up as a high-status individual, say an eight or nine out of ten, or lower, six or seven out of ten? It all depends on you and your audience.

We need to examine both our physical and *vocal* statuses when preparing to present. The volume of your voice, how loudly or softly you speak, can be another indicator of status. Ask any parent who has yelled at their kids: raising your voice when angry can have the opposite effect. Afterwards, you often don't feel great, and certainly don't feel or look like you have more status!

Raising your voice can either elevate your status or lower it. A booming voice can help people gravitate to you or be off-putting, so people move farther away. Conversely, a speaker who mumbles and is barely audible can be seen as lower status, while lowering your voice for effect so that people lean in to hear you can actually raise your status.

It doesn't matter who you are, where you are, or to whom you are presenting, being aware of your status and the status of your audience is vital to delivering a performance that engages and creates impact.

Look in the mirror or in your camera and ask yourself, "Is this the status I want to portray?" Choose your status, on the scale of one to ten, and become it physically. Once you know what status you want to present, walk on stage (literally or metaphorically), plant your feet, and deliver.

HOMEWORK

1 Stop what you are doing. Without thinking, without changing your status, take a photo or a screenshot of yourself.

2 Take a look at the photo and grade your status. Where are you on the scale? What adjustments would you make to raise your status? To lower it?

3 Now raise your status by making some decisions about how you are holding yourself and take another photo.

4 Are you happy with how you are coming across? If not, then repeat the process.

12

BODY LANGUAGE

MEET MARK BOWDEN. Mark is the world's foremost expert in body language. He's regularly called upon by the media to decode what we are seeing in the body language of celebrities or politicians. In his first book, *Winning Body Language*, Mark shares that what your body is saying and what you are saying may be two completely different things.

Mark points out that part of our brains is still reptilian in nature, which means that we have several survival instincts that kick in when we are in a moment of stress. Think about your great, great, great, great ancestors foraging for food out in the wild. If they saw or heard something, there were essentially three thoughts that went through their heads:

1 Will it eat me? Has a predator found me? Am I in danger?

2 Can I eat it? Is this going to be my dinner? I'm hungry!

3 Can I procreate with it? Can I continue to breed my species? Let's get it on!

If it's none of these three things, then it didn't even register in their world. Fascinating, right?

Walk on stage **with your hands up and out.**

When we get up to do a presentation, our reptilian brains activate. The brain communicates with us that we are at risk, that we are exposed, that we are in danger! And so we do what we would have done in the wild: we protect ourselves. We close ourselves off. We cross our arms. Or put our hands in our pockets. We look away. We make ourselves quiet. We make ourselves small.

What we want to do and what we should do are in immediate conflict. What we want to do is retreat and hide. What we need to do is open ourselves up by placing our arms out and open, so we can tell audience members and their reptilian brains that we have no tools, no weapons. By placing your hands right in front of your belly button and widening out from there you are unconsciously saying to the audience, "Everything I am telling you is the truth." Because you are speaking from the area Mark Bowden calls the Truth Plane.

In the Truth Plane, your hands and arms are in the perfect spot to make a large gesture, or as the arms go up, to signal growth or pinpoint a minute detail with a pinch in the air. With your hands in the Truth Plane, you have the freedom to move and the opportunity to connect.

It will feel odd the first time you do it, but being open—walking on stage with your hands up and out—doesn't just look good, it works! Often, when speakers come out on stage, they are nervous, so they plunge their hands into their pockets or let them hang like drooping branches down the side of their body. Picture it. Hands down at your side or in your pockets forces you to arch your back and close off your body. It immediately sets you at a lower status!

I often ask those who are resistant to walking out on stage with arms up and out to think what they would do if they were having a friend over for dinner. Your friend would knock on the door and you would greet them there, likely with your arms outstretched wide to offer them a hug or a warm handshake, and then you would gesture openly for them to come on in.

This is similar to how your favourite late-night talk show host kicks off their evening. Whether it's Jimmy Kimmel, Conan O'Brien, or Trevor Noah, these excellent entertainers always come out with arms open and out. This is *exactly* how you should be greeting the audience when you walk on stage.

The other thing all of these performers do? They find their spot. They have a little X taped on the ground, the spot they need to stand on for the best lighting, sound, and visuals. You need to do this as well.

"But, Nick, I'm not on stage, I'm in a meeting room!"

The same principle applies. Stand, walk to the front of the room, find your spot, widen your arms as you go, and welcome the crowd.

"But, Nick, I like to wander the stage or boardroom. I do my best thinking when I wander!"

Nope! Plant your feet. Find a spot. And stay there. Don't move. Wandering is distracting for your audience and, whether you know it or not, it's distracting to you too. It's the equivalent of having someone tap you on the shoulder while you're trying to talk. You lose focus. You can't do it. It's like kids tugging at Mom's or Dad's pant leg asking for something while they try to ignore them and continue talking. Wandering the stage without intention will only distract you.

"But, Nick, most of my presentations are delivered virtually while I am sitting at my desk, what can I do?"

You need to try to replicate the openness of performance when you're online as well. If you can, stand up and plant your feet. If you can't stand, that's fine, but try to cheat your hands up so the audience can see them. Imagine your belly button has moved up to your lower chest, and move your hands up to that area.

1 Choose your status.

2 Speak from the Truth Plane.

3 Plant your feet.

Claiming your space requires you to know what status you want to be in that moment and to physically hold it. It also means you need to take advantage of your arms and hands as communication tools, so you can engage with your audience on an unconscious level.

Choose your status. Speak from the Truth Plane. Plant your feet.

Here's the good news: I have shared with you two of the most common performance tips:

1   Claim your space and plant your feet.
2   Open yourself up to your audience with gesture.

In the next chapter, I share the remaining three of the top five performance tips—and it starts with your face.

HOMEWORK

1 Rehearse the opening of your talk. If you will be presenting online, then film yourself. If you will be presenting on stage, then create a practice space at home or in your office.

2 Film yourself using your phone, tablet, or laptop. This may be uncomfortable, but it's worth it!

3 Plant your feet.

4 Keep your arms open in the Truth Plane.

5 Play around with your gestures and explore other planes. Is there anything that you like?

6 Do this whole process again with a friend or partner or share your video and ask them for their thoughts. What is working? What is not?

13

YOUR FACE AND VOICE

I F THE EYES are the windows to the soul, then the smile is the doorway to your character.

Guillaume Duchenne was an eighteenth-century neurologist who studied facial expressions. Neurology did not exist in France before Duchenne, and he had an unethical way of conducting research. Using patients at a mental hospital as subjects, Duchenne produced various expressions by stimulating their facial muscles with an electrical current. The procedure was said to be extremely painful. In fact, Duchenne sometimes used the severed heads of criminals who had died by capital punishment to relieve the people with a mental health condition of the task!

Ironically, while conducting this macabre research, Guillaume uncovered something a little less dark. He identified the Duchenne smile, which involves contraction of both the zygomaticus major muscle, which raises the corners of the mouth, and the orbicularis oculi muscle, which raises the cheeks and forms crow's feet around the eyes. The Duchenne smile has been described as a smile that reaches the eyes.

The Duchenne smile is the smile we need to strive for every time we present. We know this innately, yet often when people present, a smile gets wiped from their face and a more serious, stern look takes over. This is because, unconsciously, our reptilian brain has kicked in. We feel we are at risk and since being at risk is not a pleasant experience, in addition to protecting our bodies with our arms, we put on a more serious face. The first thing that goes is our smile.

I've seen people walk out on stage with a big smile on their face. Awesome! They plant their feet and find their spot. Wicked. Then they open their mouth to speak and the smile disappears for the duration of their talk. Not good.

Some people worry that if they smile, they will be seen as fake or as a fraud. Do it anyway. A smile universally communicates happiness, and we know that happiness is contagious. When we smile, others smile back.

Smiling is something that takes a bit of work. You have to focus on creating the smile and holding it. But like all habits, once you've made it top of mind, it's an easy one to hold on to and it actually feels good! It also helps others feel good.

Now you're smiling, really smiling, and you're helping the audience smile. What about the rest of your face? Remember the eyes are the windows to the soul. We need to make eye contact with those we are speaking to.

In the '90s, Jim Carrey was a struggling stand-up comedian. He would get his brief time on stage at Yuk Yuk's in Toronto and slowly build up his act. Before his performance, he would make a habit of walking around the audience, meeting as many people as he could and shaking hands. Yes, he was networking. But more importantly, he was warming up the audience. That way, when he did take the stage, he could look out into the crowd, see some friendly faces, make eye contact, and smile. Each person in the audience thought he was connecting just with them.

While I do recommend doing a site inspection and walking the room prior to your performance or having an opportunity to connect with an audience in advance if you're pitching to

The smile is the doorway to your character.

them, this isn't always possible. Either way, making eye contact is key. And if you're presenting virtually, remember where the camera is and look at it when presenting. This is an important part of raising and keeping your status and an excellent way to build rapport with the audience.

The Three Levers of Voice: Volume, Pace, Pitch

There are a lot of incredible vocal instructors out there who can coach you on how to project your voice and improve your tone and your pitch. I want to focus on three areas that I *know* will help you to engage your audience quickly. Call them the low-hanging fruit of vocal tools. These are volume, pace, and pitch.

And all three of them are easily accessible. Think of them as levers that can be pulled quickly or even partially. Each one can provide your audience with a unique performance and engage them in a very different way. Keep in mind that your voice is a tool, an instrument you can use to help you capture and keep the audience's attention.

1. The Volume Lever

Let's start by pulling the first lever: *volume*.

Jeff Bradshaw, a leader in the international camping community and owner of the exceptional camp and outdoor centre Camp Wenonah, was my boss for many years and is now a dear friend. Back when I was a teenager during pre-camp training, I remember him telling the staff to "use their outside voice" even when they were inside. I was a theatre student back then, so I had been taught the basics about vocal projection, but I loved how Jeff put it. "Using your outside voice" doesn't mean yelling. Far from it. It just means that you speak loudly enough that even if the birds are chirping, a cabin is cheering, or a boat is zooming by, everyone can still hear you.

For some, this is not a problem. But for many, they naturally speak softly, and projecting their voice feels like yelling. I promise you, for the vast majority of you, even if you feel like you're yelling, it will not be the case.

How do we make sound from our voice? The vocal cords are attached within the larynx to the largest of the laryngeal cartilages known as the thyroid cartilage, or Adam's apple. The diaphragm is the primary muscle used in the process of breathing. This dome-shaped muscle is located just below the lungs and heart. It contracts continually as you breathe in and out. As we exhale air from the lungs, air passes through the vocal cords, which come together and begin to vibrate. This vibration produces the sound wave of your voice.

If you are struggling with how to raise your voice and not feel like you are yelling, start by planting your feet. Keep your back straight. And breathe. Let's try it.

Plant your feet.

Rest your hand gently just above your stomach on your diaphragm. And feel it fill up and empty as you breathe.

Breathe in through your nose—1, 2, 3—and out through your mouth—1, 2, 3.

Breathe in through your nose—1, 2, 3—and out through your mouth—1, 2, 3.

Breathe in through your nose—1, 2, 3—and out through your mouth—1, 2, 3.

Now say the first line of your talk—to the far side of the room.

Breathe in through your nose

1 · · · · · · · **2** · · · · · · · · **3**

and out through your mouth

1 · · · · · · · **2** · · · · · · · **3**

If you're not sure if you're projecting loudly enough, ask a friend or family member to stand at the back of the room. Did they hear you? Did it seem like you were yelling? Likely not, especially if you remembered to smile!

For some, the use of volume comes naturally, but others need to be a bit more methodical—or more like Beethoven or Bach or Vivaldi. Great composers and songwriters know that volume can help shape the experience the listener has to the music. It's called dynamics. Composers use terms related to volume to help musicians reading music understand how it's supposed to be played. For example, decrescendo means to decrease in volume; forte means loud or strong; and piano means gently or soft.

You can create some dynamics in your performance by writing down on your Communication Canvas or on your talk script exactly where you want to be louder or quieter for effect. Use the same symbols as in music notation or create your own.

Remember to breathe and always speak to the far side of the room. This will ensure that everyone will hear what you have to say.

2. The Pace Lever

We've all witnessed it: the person who races through what could have been an excellent presentation. They move so quickly that the audience starts to tune out. More often than not, this happens because the presenter's reptilian brain is kicking in, saying, "This feels risky! Get me out of here!" So unconsciously the speaker speeds up because if they speak faster, they can leave the stage sooner!

The pace or tempo of a presentation has an incredible impact on the audience and the presenter. Going back to Beethoven, here are some of the basic terms to define the overall tempo of a piece of music: allegro is lively or quick;

andante is a moderate tempo; presto is very fast; and lento is slow. Each term has its own symbol in musical notation, which you can use or you can make up your own. I have had executives mark up their presentation scripts with their own symbols for volume and pace. That way when they are rehearsing, they can practice increasing or slowing down their pace to help . . . drive . . . home . . . important . . . messages!

The Power of the Pause

I want to stop here and touch on the power of the pause. Turning the volume off.

In early 2020, COVID-19 was sweeping the world, causing thousands of deaths, wreaking havoc on our economy, and triggering all kinds of damage to our mental health and well-being. The planes were grounded. Offices closed. Restaurants and bars went dark. The music stopped. Some called it "The Great Pause."

I have just mentioned a few of the negative effects of the Great Pause. But some wonderful things happened too: new ideas, innovations, inventions. Books were written, including this one. Music was written and recorded. The creative output was unlike anything the world has ever seen before.

According to an article in *Harvard Business Review* written by three authors who conducted a meta-analysis of 145 studies on constraints, while people tend to believe constraints stifle creativity, they actually have the opposite effect.[1] The reason for this burst of creativity and productiveness during the pandemic was that when we stopped, we could think. We had time to reflect. We had time to create.

The same is true when you are presenting. Pausing helps you think. It helps you reflect. It helps you create.

If you find that you are racing through your presentation do the following: Pause. Breathe. Smile.

Pause.

Breathe.

Smile.

The pause will do two things. It will help you by giving you some space to determine where you want to go, and it will help your audience by providing them some time to catch up. Remember that they don't know your content like you do!

Just as a loud noise shocks the system, a pause can get everyone's attention. If you are speaking and someone in the room is looking at their phone, checking their email, or even writing a note, the pause will get their attention. They will stop and look up to see what they've missed. Try it.

Warming Up

When someone is speaking too quickly, it often becomes difficult to follow what they are saying, and their meaning becomes jumbled. In order to truly pace yourself, you need to enunciate each word clearly. And to do this, you need to warm up your mouth and tongue.

"Nick, how on earth do I warm up my mouth and tongue?" Ask Peter of "Peter Piper picked a peck of pickled peppers" fame. That's right. Saying tongue twisters out loud can help with pace *and* clarity! I recommend using a few different tongue twisters that focus on different areas of the mouth and tongue.

- To warm up your lips, repeat the following five times slowly, then five times quickly: "Peter Piper picked a peck of pickled peppers" or "Unique New York."

- To warm up your tongue, repeat the following five times slowly, then five times quickly: "The tip of the tongue on the teeth and the lips" or "Red leather, yellow leather."

If you find it challenging, start slowly and keep trying. Continue to breathe and try smiling! As you improve, slowly pick up the pace.

3. The Pitch Lever

Pitch is tricky because it requires us to be more aware of our voice and how others hear it. Pitch is a perceived fundamental frequency of sound while tone is the "quality" of that sound. As already mentioned, when we get nervous, we tend to speed up. This increase in pace means that less air is coming from our lungs and through our vocal cords. When we have less air coming out, our tone and pitch changes.

For inexperienced presenters or those who get nervous, this lack of air can result in what some people call "uptalk." Made famous in the 1980s as the sound of the "Valley Girl," uptalk is characterized by a rise in pitch at the end of sentences, resulting in a consistent interrogative sound. This results in a tone of inexperience—it sounds like you don't know what you're talking about.

For example, read this passage again but with each sentence ending as a question. Your intonation will go up at the end of every sentence.

For inexperienced presenters who are nervous, this lack of air can result in what some people call "uptalk"? Made famous in the 1980s as the sound of the "Valley Girl," uptalk is characterized by a rise in pitch at the end of sentences, resulting in a consistent interrogative sound? This results in a tone of inexperience—it sounds like you don't know what you're talking about?

Another common and more current tone challenge is what is called "vocal fry." Vocal fry describes a specific sound quality caused by the movement of the vocal folds. In regular speaking mode, "the vocal folds rapidly... as the air comes through. That popping, jittery effect gives it a characteristic sizzling or frying sound."[2] Think Kim Kardashian saying... pretty much anything!

Unlike uptalk, which is often interpreted as a sign of a lack of intelligence, vocal fry is seen as raising the status of speakers among certain groups. This might be why more and more people are embracing it. That being said, for any professional talk, vocal fry is distracting.

So, how do you fix the uptalk and vocal fry?

Breathing. That's right, relaxing your breathing will help you to slow down and pass more air from the lungs, through your vocal cords, and out your mouth.

Here's how to relax your breathing:

1 Stand up straight, with your feet shoulder width apart.

2 Keep your back straight and your chin slightly raised.

3 Place one hand or both hands just above your stomach or diaphragm.

4 Breathe in for a three count: 1, 2, 3, pause. Your stomach should be raised and full.

5 Breathe out for a three count: 1, 2, 3, pause.

6 Do this three times and then say your first line, slowly. The more air you can feed your voice, the better the tone.

Before you shake off this touchy-feely exercise, I want to tell you about James. From the age of five, James was raised by his maternal grandparents on their farm in Jackson, Michigan. James found the transition to living with his grandparents in Michigan traumatic and developed a stutter so severe that he refused to speak. Eventually, a teacher helped him overcome his stutter, but he remained functionally mute for eight years until he entered high school.

One day, James's high school English teacher, Mr. Crouch, made him read one of his poems aloud to the class. James already knew the verses very well and shocked himself by reading them aloud perfectly without a hint of a stutter! Needless to say, Mr. Crouch was quite pleased and told James that they would use his poetry to reclaim his speech. Mr. Crouch began to function as a de facto speech therapist. Throughout the rest of high school, James practised talking by reading Shakespeare and Poe aloud. He also participated in dramatic reading and debating classes.

James is James Earl Jones, who went on to become one of the most memorable voices on the planet. He is the voice of Darth Vader in the Star Wars film franchise and the voice of Mufasa from *The Lion King*, and he's the announcer who says, "This is CNN." One of the greatest voice actors ever overcame a speech impediment by breathing and reading aloud. He couldn't just get up and deliver. He had to practice.

And so do you. The Three Levers of Voice—volume, pace, and pitch—are easy to access and can make a huge difference to your delivery. Don't forget to use them.

HOMEWORK

1   Take a selfie not smiling. Then take a selfie with your best Duchenne smile. Ask yourself, "Which facial expression would I rather have when starting a presentation?"

2   When in conversation today, choose to play with your Three Levers of Voice. Try adjusting your volume slightly, then do the same with your pace and pitch.

3   Review your presentation and write down your own dynamics for volume, pace, and pitch using musical notation or your own symbols. Use a pencil so you can erase or adjust later.

14

REHEARSE, REHEARSE, REHEARSE

LOVE JAZZ MUSIC. My parents brought me up listening to the greats, from Miles Davis to Louis Armstrong to Billie Holiday to Ella Fitzgerald. Each one of them held mastery over their instrument and over whatever piece of music they were performing.

If you play an instrument, you'll know what I am talking about. If you know the song well, no matter what happens—a car honking, a baby crying, the *Titanic* sinking—you can continue to play without distraction. Or you can take what you have created and make it even better. Or truly original.

When Jimi Hendrix performed "The Star-Spangled Banner" at Woodstock, blowing the minds of not just attendees but the world, he took something so familiar and completely reinvented it musically and dramatically. He couldn't have done it without knowing the song inside and out. The same is true with your presentation. Let's take stock:

You have filled out your Communication Canvas; embraced the power of story, used the Story Spine and rhetorical devices throughout; created slides that sparkle but don't outshine you; learned how to claim your space and use status, gesture, and body language to help you do that; and learned how to use your facial expression and voice to connect with your audience.

YOU HAVE:

☑ **filled out your Communication Canvas**

☑ **embraced the power of story, used the Story Spine and rhetorical devices throughout**

☑ **created slides that sparkle but don't outshine you**

☑ **learned how to claim your space and use status, gesture, and body language to help you do that**

☑ **learned how to use your facial expression and voice to connect with your audience**

It's time to present, right? Not. So. Fast.

You need to ensure that you know your content inside and out. Only then will you know *when* you're going to gesture, *when* to adjust your voice, *which* slides you are going to use and when, and *how* you're going to close.

In short, you need to practice.

The more comfortable you are with your content, the more flexible you will be delivering it. And it's at this point that I want to let you in on a little secret. If you are presenting, you are a performer. If you are running a meeting, you are a performer. If you are meeting someone for a sales meeting or a job interview, you are a performer.

And to get yourself ready for your performance, you need to rehearse. You need to practice going over your talk, your pitch, or your presentation again and again and again.

Rehearsal Techniques

Memory

I have a very bad memory. Even though I've been on stage and on TV, my memory's probably the thing that has caused me the most anxiety. Will I remember my lines? I have a vivid recollection of being on stage with my troupe and completely blanking on what I was going to say. James and Todd were waiting for me to say my line and kept giving me cues. It was awful.

But at the same time, I'm still here. Meaning, although the experience was dreadful and it has left an indelible mark on my memory, I lived through it. It prompted me to work on my memorization even harder. It has encouraged me to develop a system and a process to help me prepare for any performance.

Time

The first thing you need to be successful in preparing for any presentation or performance is time. The more time you have, the more you can rehearse! So plan ahead and be kind to yourself. Give yourself the time you need to succeed.

Colour

During my program, when I first introduce the Communication Canvas, I share it as an image of colourful blocks. (You can download a colour version at impactbook.ca/tools.) Each block represents a key element of your talk from the Lean In Moment to the Close. The blocks are colour-coded because each one can be created, tangibly, in the real world, on either a Post-it Note or a cue card. So when your Communication Canvas is ready, transcribe the content from the page to your colour-coded cards or Post-its.

Repetition

Start by leaving those cards out across the table while you rehearse. I start my first run-throughs by saying the talk out loud from beginning to end while looking at the cards.

Raise to Eye Level

Once you've done this two or three times, take the cards and put them on the wall at eye level. Find a wall that you can tape them to (or if they're Post-its, stick them to) and again, ensure that the cards are at eye level.

Repetition. Again.

Now I want you to repeat the process. Rehearse by staring at the cards on the wall, following the Communication Canvas that you've constructed. Do this another three or four times.

If you are presenting,
you are a performer.

If you are running a meeting,
you are a performer.

If you are meeting
someone for a sales
meeting or a job interview,
you are a performer.

The word "rehearse" derives from the twelfth-century Old French word *rehercier*, which means "to go over again, repeat." That's the best thing you can do to help yourself not just remember but get more comfortable with your content. By going through the colour-coded Communication Canvas (add that to your tongue twister warm-up), you are creating an unconscious association with your content and the colour of the card. This will help you remember what is coming next. Think of it as a colourful road map of the content.

Finally, by moving the cards up to the wall, you have fully evolved, from writing and prepping to standing and rehearsing. You are now practising with your back straight, standing in place, arms outstretched. This is the way you should look when you are rehearsing. All you are missing is an audience.

I have seen this approach work wonders for many speakers, including myself. A few years ago, during one of my speaking intensives, Kim, a senior programmer from a growing tech firm, was delivering her final talk. The four-day retreat culminated with each participant delivering a ten-minute talk to a live audience and Kim was crushing it. Her talk was about how improvisational thinking was the lifeblood of technological innovation. It was fascinating.

She delivered great content and a solid performance, and she was very happy. After she finished, I remember chatting and congratulating her on her talk. I asked her how she felt.

"Relieved. I had a moment in there where I totally blanked. I forgot where I was."

"Really?" I said. "When? I couldn't tell!"

"I was about to transition into my second Essential Message and I went blank. I panicked for a moment. And then I turned my head. I had been rehearsing in my hotel room, with the cards up on the wall. I could see them. I could see the red card! I knew what was on it. And I continued from there."

REHEARSE, REHEARSE, REHEARSE 199

I loved it. I told her I had thought that moment was simply an effective use of the dramatic pause. No one noticed a thing!

That is the impact of using these rehearsal techniques. The moment you need it most, the content will be there. So use the Communication Canvas to envision the outline in your mind as you rehearse.

Record Yourself!

We all have a smartphone or access to one, so take the time to record yourself, either just audio or video. When I was preparing for my TEDx Talk, I used both. It's easy—except once you've recorded yourself, you have to go through the painful process of listening to yourself.

The first few times you listen to your talk, I recommend having a notebook or a draft of your talk handy. You will hear things you want to change! You can makes notes to adjust and fix things after you've listened to the talk.

Once you've incorporated changes, you will need to rerecord the talk. No point in listening to an older draft. You can take this audio recording on the road. Listen to it while you are out for a walk, while running, or driving. I know some speakers who have listened to a recording of themselves while they are going to bed.

I used to run and listen to myself. I would listen all the way down the trail and recite it by memory all the way back.

Pre-COVID, Dr. Molly Shoichet told me that she would walk from her office down busy Yonge Street in Toronto speaking her presentation aloud. The street was full of people, some on their phones. She didn't worry about what she looked like.

If there is one overall, pervading message of this chapter, here it is: rehearse, rehearse, rehearse. Find the time and do it a variety of different ways.

We should never be striving for perfection. **We should always be striving for *progress*.**

Practise in Chunks or in Reverse Order

Only do the opening. Then only focus on an Essential Message. You decide. If you can deliver it out of order, then you are really mastering your talk. A great way to ensure you know your content? Deliver the talk from back to front.

Remove the Cards and Your Visuals

Get rid of any visual support and practise your presentation. Again, those things are simply speaker support—you don't need them to deliver the talk.

Finally, I will let you in on the most important thing you need to know about forgetting your content: it doesn't matter.

Don't get me wrong. It matters to *you*. And it matters if you are sharing something that isn't factually correct. But the little bump or the moment of forgetting your place—it truly doesn't matter.

To paraphrase Voltaire, "perfect is the enemy of good."

We should never be striving for perfection. We should always be striving for *progress*. So when you forget your spot or mispronounce a word, you are learning. You have the opportunity to recognize what happened and grow.

Please, please, please do not beat yourself up by trying to deliver the perfect talk. There is no such thing as the perfect talk. There is only your idea. And you need to share it with the world.

HOMEWORK

Your talk deadline is likely coming up. So now you need to:

1 Allocate enough time for rehearsal. Make sure you block it into your calendar.

2 Rehearse. Rehearse. Rehearse.

3 Try the technique of using colour-coded cards on the table, then up on the wall.

4 Repeat as many times as you can.

5 Record and listen to yourself.

6 Finally, ask a friend to listen and get their feedback.

CONCLUSION: TIME TO DELIVER

AM NOT A religious person, but I do feel reverence for those who take the time to develop their ideas and share them with the world. My good friend Ron Tite is one of the most successful and sought-after keynote speakers in North America. He's the author of two books (*Think. Do. Say.* and *Everyone's an Artist*), he owns a successful content marketing agency, and he speaks more than sixty times a year to some of the world's biggest brands.

A few years ago we were out for dinner for his birthday. Over wine and steak, he shared a wonderful philosophy for enhancing his talks, which he calls the model car and the assembly line.

Most model cars never get made. A whole lot of time and money go into developing new designs, new technologies, and new approaches to building a model car. These models often get unveiled and people get excited about certain aspects of them.

"Oh! I like the heated windshield wipers!" "The tinted windows based on the time of the day is a cool feature!" "Hands-free radio is a game changer!"

For every one of those items the team loves, there are literally hundreds of features that seem either unimportant or

Keep presenting. Keep creating.

Keep presenting. **Keep creating.**

Keep presenting. Keep creating.

Keep presenting. **Keep creating.**

Keep presenting. Keep creating.

Keep presenting. **Keep creating.**

Keep presenting. Keep creating.

Keep presenting. **Keep creating.**

Keep presenting. Keep creating.

Keep presenting. **Keep creating.**

Keep presenting. Keep creating.

Keep presenting. **Keep creating.**

Keep presenting. Keep creating.

Keep presenting. **Keep creating.**

impossible to achieve, because it would involve rebuilding the plant or assembly line, at huge cost. But there are always one or two items that make it. The hands-free radio and the heated wipers are small and easy enough to manufacture that they get added to the assembly line. That's why the next year's model has some pretty nifty features that the previous year's did not.

Ron believes we need to build towards our dream talks by going out and delivering presentations that consist of the stuff we know works—but every time we present, we should add a small percentage of new content. You have to try out a few nifty features to see if they land. If they don't, oh well! You tried and you can put them out to pasture.

But if they do work, if the audience is engaged, smiling, laughing, or asking questions about the content, then it goes into your assembly line. It now becomes a part of your content moving forward.

Keep presenting. Keep creating.

If you've developed one great talk, keep sharing it with the world. But at the same time, please keep creating more talks, more content. You have the tools to create a talk, a pitch, a presentation that can engage any audience and you don't want to stay in the same place delivering the same content forever. I know that you have ideas that are percolating inside you. Take the time to articulate those ideas, share them with others, and keep going.

My mission is to work with people who have forgotten about stories. From ophthalmologists to blockchain consultants to regenerative medicine scientists to innovative business leaders to students, I consistently remind them of their power as storytellers.

Once they understand how to share purpose, unique ideas, or complex information through story, they experience two things. First, they are amazed at how story can help them have real impact. Then they get excited. Very excited.

Today is a gift. Communication is a gift.

———————————

Try it. In your next email, meeting, phone call, pitch, or presentation, whatever your communication, start with purpose and simplify your content by using structure, transform your content by sharing a story, and perform your message with confidence. You will begin to engage others in a way you never imagined before. You will connect and drive towards your desired impact.

Remember that a small idea shared repeatedly has tremendous power.

Not long ago I was out with my running crew on a long run. You can have good runs and bad ones, and I was having a bad one. I was complaining about something. My foot hurt. And my friend Mary responded, "Today's a gift."

It wasn't the first time she'd said this. I loved the quote. But that day I asked her who said it. I was expecting someone like Gandhi or Mother Teresa.

She turned to me and, without skipping a beat, said, "Master Oogway. From *Kung Fu Panda*."

The full quotation is "Yesterday is history. Tomorrow is a mystery. But today is a gift. That is why it is called the present." I have since sourced the quote from either Eleanor Roosevelt or Bill Keane.

Today is a gift.

I would also say, "*Communication* is a gift." And it's a gift we take for granted because communication is hard work. But when you take the time, carefully package up your knowledge and ideas, wrap it up in a story, and share it with the world, you are doing something very special. When you share that gift, others will receive it and then they'll share it too. They will build upon your story.

Communication is hard work, but it can be learned.

Whether you're a student, someone just starting their career, or an expert who has been working for years, your ability to authentically communicate and connect with others is a differentiator that will shape your success. Because it's not money that makes the world go 'round, it's communication.

And when done right, it can make the world a better place.

HOMEWORK

1 Go and deliver your talk.

2 Revise your talk based on audience feedback.

3 Start work on your next talk.

4 Keep going. The world needs your ideas.

5 Share your talk with me at impactbook.ca!

ACKNOWLEDGEMENTS

S WITH MOST projects of passion, this book has been a journey, and it couldn't have been created without the help of many important people.

I want to thank my incredibly talented and supportive wife, Helen, for her undying support through the years, but more specifically over the last year while I have been writing this book. I also want to thank my children, Noah and Sarah, who have tolerated my intermittent absences while I delivered my speaker coaching programs abroad, and patiently (and impatiently) experienced me sneaking a communication lesson in over the dinner table. Every absence and every conversation have helped me refine the process and thinking that made it into this book.

I want to thank my mother, Rosalind Kindler, for always believing in me and teaching me the power of storytelling from an early age. Thank you to my brother, Damian Kindler, for always being my biggest fan and my closest friend. Both my mother and brother are incredible writers and inspired me to step forward, put pen to paper, and create!

Heartfelt thanks and appreciation to the endlessly talented Ron Tite for sharing his thoughts in the Foreword. Beyond being a dear friend for more than thirty years, he is also an inspiration to me as a writer, entrepreneur, and speaker.

I want to thank Oren Berkovich, Krista Pawley, and the team at SingularityU Canada and BePossible for being such tremendous partners and believing in the power of speaker coaching!

To all the scientists and specialists I have worked with at MaRS Discovery District, University of Toronto Department of Ophthalmology, Boston Children's Hospital, Medicine by Design, and many more—thank you! Thank you for pushing yourselves and challenging the status quo.

Sincere and deep appreciation goes to Debbie Gamble; Clint Mahlman, Rob Felix, and others from London Drugs; Dr. Molly Shoichet; Dr. David Hunter; Floyd Marinescu; Dr. Afsaneh Alavi; and all my valued clients (far too many to mention here!). Thank you for believing in the coaching process and the power of storytelling.

I want to thank team at Page Two for their partnership and support. You made this dream a reality and made it fun too!

And thank you to all of you who continue to create, inspire, dream, and share! Keep going. Keep sharing. Keep communicating. You make our world a better place!

NOTES

Introduction

1   See Institute for Healthcare Communication, "Impact of Communication in Healthcare" (July 2011), healthcarecomm.org/about-us/impact-of-communication-in-healthcare; and Amgad Makaryus and Eli Friedman, "Patients' Understanding of Their Treatment Plans and Diagnosis at Discharge," *Mayo Clinic Proceedings* 80, no. 8 (2005), doi.org/10.4065/80.8.991.

2   Andrew S. Epstein et al., "Discussions of Life Expectancy and Changes in Illness Understanding in Patients with Advanced Cancer," *Journal of Clinical Oncology* 34, no. 20 (July 10, 2016), doi.org/10.1200/JCO.2015.63.6696.

1: The Path to Impact

1   World Health Organization, "Diabetes" fact sheet (June 8, 2020), who.int/news-room/fact-sheets/detail/diabetes.

2: Your Idea Matters

1   Marianne Williamson, *A Return to Love: Reflections on the Principles of A Course In Miracles* (New York: HarperPerennial, 1993).

4: An Ending to Remember

1   Erik Larson, *The Splendid and the Vile: A Saga of Churchill, Family, and Defiance during the Blitz* (New York: Crown, 2020).

2   Tim Weiner, "R.V. Jones, Science Trickster Who Foiled Nazis, Dies at 86," *New York Times* (December 19, 1997), nytimes.com/1997/12/19/us/r-v-jones-science-trickster-who-foiled-nazis-dies-at-86.html.

5: Why Story Matters

1   Tim O'Brien, *The Things They Carried* (New York: Houghton Mifflin, 1990).

2   Cody Delistraty, "The Psychological Comforts of Storytelling," *The Atlantic* (November 2, 2014), theatlantic.com/health/archive/2014/11/the-psychological-comforts-of-storytelling/381964.

3   Gordon Bower and Michal Clark, "Narrative Stories as Mediators for Serial Learning," *Psychonomic Science* 14, nos. 181–82 (April 1969), doi.org/10.3758/BF03332778.

4   As cited in Annie Murphy Paul, "Your Brain on Fiction," *New York Times* (March 17, 2012), nytimes.com/2012/03/18/opinion/sunday/the-neuroscience-of-your-brain-on-fiction.html.

7: The Power of Emotional Language

1   A video of Dr. Martin Luther King Jr.'s full "I Have a Dream" speech is available on YouTube (youtu.be/c_nvqRqTiKk), or listen to a recording at NPR: npr.org/2010/01/18/122701268/i-have-a-dream-speech-in-its-entirety.

13: Your Face and Voice

1   Oguz Acar et al., "Why Constraints Are Good for Innovation," *Harvard Business Review* (November 22, 2019), hbr.org/2019/11/why-constraints-are-good-for-innovation.

2   Arika Okrent, "What Is Vocal Fry?" *Mental Floss* (August 24, 2018), mentalfloss.com/article/61552/what-vocal-fry.

ABOUT THE AUTHOR

K EYNOTE SPEAKER, communication coach, and eternal entrepreneur Nick Kindler works with leaders, entrepreneurs, scientists, and academics to become stronger, more effective communicators and speakers. A passionate advocate for innovation and communication, Nick was the head of programming at SingularityU Canada, a former coach and director of programming at TEDxToronto, and is the cofounder of speaker agency Talk Boutique. As founder and CEO of Kindler and Company, he provides transformational learning experiences that help leaders become better communicators.

YOUR NEXT STEPS ON THE PATH TO IMPACT

Tools

Find further resources and downloadables for all the tools mentioned in this book—the Three Step Purpose Practice, Communication Canvas, Story Spine, and more—at impactbook.ca/tools.

Takeaways

What's your biggest takeaway from this book? Are you inspired to write a review? If you have gleaned some wisdom, learned a new technique, or found new, valuable insights in these pages, please consider

- Giving this book a five-star review on your favourite online retailer.

- Sharing this book with your closest big-brained friends to help them become better communicators.

- Getting copies of this book for your management team or leaders within your organization to help improve the quality of communication from the very top.

- Sending us a message at impactbook.ca. Have a great presentation story or idea to help make presentations a success? We'd love to hear from you.

- Using it! Go forth and communicate with impact using these processes and techniques.

Next Steps

Get further, faster on your journey to impact. Kindler and Company offers programs, workshops, and personalized coaching and consulting. Learn more and sign up at kindlerandcompany.com.

1 **JOIN THE GLOBAL ONLINE COMMUNITY**
Learn from passionate thinkers, speakers, leaders, and communicators who want to stand out. Become a part of the global conversation on how to communicate with impact.

2 **ONLINE TRAINING**
Sign up for a variety of video programs:

THREE STEP PURPOSE PRACTICE
A walk-through of the best way to create a solid Purpose Statement.

SIMPLIFY AND TRANSFORM
A step-by-step process of how to build a simplified talk structure and integrate storytelling into your presentation.

THINK LIKE A PERFORMER
Now that you've created your talk, it's time to think like a performer. Here we dig into all the elements of performance covered in the book, and then some, showing you how to put your best foot forward.

3 IMPACT ACCELERATOR
Learn how to use the tools and techniques from impact coaches and selected speakers. Every month, experience live group workshops and group coaching sessions as we explore all the tools in the toolbelt and introduce new ones.

4 APPLY FOR THE IMPACT PROGRAM
Every quarter, Kindler and Company selects a group of twenty leaders from around the world to participate in the Impact Program. These sessions are designed to take you from a germ of an idea to TEDx-stage-worthy talk over the course of a few short months.